LOVE TRACKS

LOVE TRACKS
MYSTICAL ADVENTURES IN THE COMPANY OF DOGS

D.J. FILSON

Humanics Trade Group
Lake Worth, FL

HUMANICS

Love Tracks
A Humanics Trade Group Publication
© 2006 by Brumby Holdings, Inc.
First Edition

Humanics Trade Group Publications is an imprint of and published by Humanics Publishing Group, a division of Brumby Holdings, Inc. Its trademark, consisting of the words "Humanics Trade Group" and the portrayal of a pegasus, is registered in the U.S. Patent and Trademark Office and in other countries.

Cover photo by D.J. Filson.

Brumby Holdings, Inc.
12 S. Dixie Hwy, Ste. 203
Lake Worth, FL 33460
USA

Printed in the United States of America and the United Kingdom

ISBN (Paperback) 0-89334-417-6
ISBN (Hardcover) 0-89334-418-4

Library of Congress Control Number: 2006924350

For Sofie

and all the dogs that I have loved,

both present and beyond.

TABLE OF CONTENTS

FOREWORD

Love Tracks made me smile, cry, laugh, and cherish the memories of the wonderful animals that have passed through my life. Animals, wild and domestic, have given me strength and courage where I thought there was none. They exude a calm, intelligent and loving presence that draws me to them. Our animal companions show us how to observe and experience the world around us with open hearts, minds and souls. They live each moment to the fullest. If we choose, we could learn so much from our pets.

In *Love Tracks,* Dorothy explores the roles that animals play in our lives. How they can help us with the acceptance of good and bad in the world. Her stories, quotes, and personal insights are inspirational and emotionally fulfilling. I found myself reflecting on my life as a veterinarian and the animals that have touched my heart and soul. These animals brought compassion, understanding, patience, and unconditional love to the people who shared their lives. There have been many times in my career that animals have come back against all odds to health and well-being. We should live so happily and be so content.

Love Tracks is an insightful investigation into the human animal bond through spirituality. Thank you, Dorothy, for giving us an opportunity to search for the peaceful being in all of us.

Kari Swenson, D.V.M.

ACKNOWLEDGMENTS

For their unending support and belief in me, I thank my parents, Velma and Henry, and my two stalwart brothers, Bill and Tom. Because of them, I shared a solid family unit--a steady, balanced childhood base from which to launch my improbable, but compelling dreams and aspirations.

Deep gratitude goes to Gary Wilson, chairman at Humanics Publishing Group for his belief in this project and his mutual enthusiasm for West Highland White Terriers. Muchas gracias to Carol Kuchera for her unwavering encouragement and feedback on this book, from its genesis to the toast of achievement.

Many individuals have provided the foundation from which this book evolved. Some shared the adventures depicted in this book and other have provided the deep interest and attention that is evident in a friend. For those, a special note of appreciation: Buzz "Helen" McCartney, Nancy Loren, Sharon Reidy Toussaint, Lissa Barber, Darcy Saunders, Dia Winograd, Jan Ullom, Selma Putnam, and Karen Emerson,

And, for sharing their dog stories: Myrna Williams, Greg Leichner, James Emmel, Carolynne Jones, Jo Jorgensen, Trish Kinley, Bonnie Mueller, Judy Bystrom, and animal advocate extraordinaire, Patt Nichols.

May we always remember the blessings that our animal friends bring to our lives and to this planet. They help us develop an appreciation of things unseen. The essense is slowly absorbed from other realms; the knowingness comes from other than the direct senses. Yet, the realness feels just as strong, perhaps more so because we have trusted the unknown, and it has delivered.

A special blessing to little Sofie, Cuya, Scruff, Little Bear, Griz, Mister, Kobuk, Laddie, Lick, all of Cuya's beautiful puppies and sweet Sadie.

In dedication to our noble co-species, a portion of the proceeds of this book will be donated to the American Humane Society and the American Society for the Prevention to Cruelty to Animals.

D. J. Filson
Bozeman, Montana

INTRODUCTION

Comparing the noble qualities of our canine companions with the attributes of those individuals who, throughout centuries of spiritual evolution, have been identified as mystics, is an endeavor that has been skirted by authors and scholars over the years but never fully explored. The characteristics held in common by these two esteemed groups are well known and firmly established. It is widely acknowledged that both circles freely demonstrate love, acceptance, and a propensity to contemplate. And then they act on their profound beliefs. Writers, enthused by one coterie or the other, can enumerate, at length, their remarkably positive and inspiring traits. But what do these two circles have in common, and is there anything to be gained by exploring this connection?

Dogs and mystics. How do they compare? Do they possess features of such merit that by observing them, interacting with them, and measuring them side by side, we might discover qualities—an essence to emulate—that could bring peace and comfort to our highly complicated, stress-filled lives?

Upon examining both groups in general, we know the following: their principal life-guiding emotion is love. For them, joy is often found in ordinary life experiences and they (dogs and mystics alike) are content to live simply, in the present moment. They are legendary in their loyalty, bestowing unconditional regard towards their companions and acquaintances. They impart forgiveness and sacrifice for the common good in an authentic, all encompassing desire to give. They relish each moment, rather than worrying and waiting (suspending their joy) until life becomes perfect.

Both groups practice contemplation; it appears to aid them, through solitude and silence, in discovering and accessing their true natures. Through this process, they develop an inner strength (founded on self-knowledge), courage, and clarity of purpose. The proportion of their happiness is measured, to a great degree, by their sense of inter-connectedness to their surroundings, to other beings. By maintaining a sensitivity and compassion to the world around them, they exude spon-taneity and creativity, and inspire honesty and good humor. But, the true measure of their success is their ability to both give and receive love.

As is often the case with paradigm shifts, my own pursuit of this subject stemmed from a major, life-changing event—in my case, a tragedy. On January 11, 2000, as darkness fell and dusk recast into night, my beloved West Highland Terrier, Sofie, slipped through the ice on the creek that runs through our back yard and drowned. Sofie was an excellent swimmer, a grand adventurer who loved the water. But, the combination of darkness, frigid conditions, and becoming trapped beneath the dense ice was too extreme for even her brave and daring countenance to overcome.

What began for her as one last creek-side exploration before darkness fell, ended with her vibrant young life extinguished in the cold, dark water.

Sofie and I spent as much time as possible near the creek. It was my refuge, a place to read and write, and simply enjoy the resplendence of nature. For Sofie, whose very name connotes the cosmic wisdom which abides in all creatures and permeates the Universe, it was a won-derland of rippling water, lush range grass, teeming with wildlife, fil-tered light, and absorbing scents.

One afternoon, the previous summer, as we had enjoyed the exquisite murmur of flowing water, blended with bird songs and creaking branches, a solitary sandhill crane touched down directly across the creek, less than thirty feet from us. The crane, satisfied at finding such a lush respite of tall grass, ferns, and shade from the lofty evergreens, drew in its massive wings and began preening its fawn-colored breast feathers. Indeed, it was as large as a fawn. We watched, enraptured, obliged for this enchanted moment.

Finally, when it noticed us, the great bird reassessed the situation. It began its ascent, slowly charging its massive, rhythmic wingspan, extending slowly into flight to gain the loft needed to clear the dense tree-line. Mesmerized, we watched as it carved a graceful, giant arc in the sky above, and finally, made one last pass directly over our heads, as if to bid us adieu and find a more private resting place. Experiences like this, shared with this dynamic little dog, made Sofie's presence in my life a treasure, a blessing I will hold with me forever.

But that stormy, winter night, after what seemed an eternity of breaking through the dense ice in fear and desperation, battling the waist-deep, freezing water, and overhanging willows in the dark, I had her in my arms again, but not in time to save her life.

In the days and nights that followed I felt numb, confused, misplaced, and empty. The reality of what had occurred seemed profoundly unreal. Sofie had been such a vital and loving support to me; shock and grief shrouded my days and nights. Food held no interest. I could scarcely breathe. Sleep came only in erratic, restless jags; I loathed being alone. At times, I feared that I, too, might be swept away into a dark, cold void. Tears and fears and a deep longing to see her sweet face, to smell her sweet scent once again, veiled each day.

Those who have ever grieved, know that when our hearts are ripped open, beyond any protection the mind can offer, we are forced to face the raw reality of life (and death), just as it is. We become acutely aware of the superficial nature of many of our concerns and distractions, mourning lost opportunities, tinged with regret. This is a truth that cannot be altered or ignored. Life as we knew it will never be the same.

Major changes, and certainly every death we experience, offer important lessons, if we can somehow find a way to meet the pain, and remain open to receive them. Each insight we gain becomes a permanent part of us, unique and profound, one that we will not have to learn again. As we struggle with the loss, pain, sadness, exhaustion, disbelief, and anger, we shed an old self. We are changed forever. This time of transformation can impart a valuable new awareness. To resist it, although a natural, instinctive response, is futile and ultimately contrary to the natural order. To truly heal, we must *surrender*, and eventually, learn to recognize the good that counterbalances the trauma. Knowing that any day could be our last, or that of a loved one, helps us focus on the precious potential of each moment and to treasure each one. We can allow ourselves to feel gratitude for the special gifts our departed friends visited upon our lives, and pay tribute to the goodness they bestowed on us.

Death is the most dramatic change we will ever face, and when it touches our lives we learn that change, like death, is inevitable. The more we resist change, the longer we remain immobilized in the confines of our perceived limitations. We do, however, possess the fortitude and resources necessary to manage any situation; we merely need to discover and activate them. This process can lead to profound growth and wisdom as we become more aware, more dynamic, more responsive to Life and its infinite possibilities.

One endeavor that had helped me many times in the past to deal with pain and uncertainty was to revisit my collection of inspirational and life-affirming books. This collection, a perennial "work in progress", contains the thoughts and guidance of a wide array of astute teachers and writers. Many of these books had been recommended by enlightened friends, confidantes who successfully negotiated their own daring quests through life. Pouring through them is like meeting a cadre of familiar old friends. The experience generates feelings of comfort, hope and reassurance. Words, that once provided guidance through trials of the past, are resurrected to aid in a new context. Many of the old tomes are highlighted, dog-eared, and worn from numerous readings, the margins filled with comments and interpretations.

During the weeks following Sofie's departure, a perennial favorite, Marsha Sinetar's *Ordinary People as Monks and Mystics*, somehow made its way to the top of the pile. I peruse it every few years and always manage to extract some new wisdom, a fresher perspective that helps bring focus and a sense of faith to my stress-filled, fractured world. I hoped, in abounding sorrow, that this small book of wisdom could help make sense of Sofie's death—to bring some meaning and solace to a seemingly senseless event—one that I continued to rage against.

As I read it again, I found myself focusing on the qualities that mark a mystic. Thoughts of love, joyfulness, the ability to forgive, the capacity for contemplation and profound loyalty swirled in my head and merged with the ever present grief I felt for Sofie. Then, one day, a revelation: *Sofie was a mystic!* And all of my other remarkable dog friends throughout my life had been mystics! It seemed so clear; they had so much in common that (except for the fur and four legs) it was hard to tell one from the other.

And, upon reflection, it was clear: Sofie's time on earth was the embodiment of a life lived fully. She knew her desires and would not be held back. She recognized her path and heeded it with all her heart. And, when her journey was complete, God sent an owl to redeem her, and gathered her soul back home. She merged with something larger than herself, and became one with the Light.

And, thus, began my journey to sort through this mystery more thoroughly. I wanted more evidence, if that was possible. This discovery provided me with a measure of comfort that I hoped to confirm. I wanted to pass on to others a whisper of what it means to be touched by the profound gifts that dogs have to offer.

Our courageous companions, joyful, loving, forgiving, and non-judgmental, prevail and exalt in the present. Their affections towards us are both unpretentious and accepting, allowing us to be our true selves in a soft glow of humility.

If we follow our canine teachers' fine examples of courage, strength, tenderness, loyalty, and love, our reward will be the gift of grace. Dogs are at ease with spontaneous, authentic moments; their approach to life's events is not dominated by the logic to which we humans often succumb. They achieve a greater participation in life as they draw upon all their senses. In addition to the intangible, the capacity to protect, to intuit, and to be patient, dogs truly live in the present moment, and authentically experience all that life has to offer. They are our steady friends, warm, reliable, light-hearted, and supportive. They share our achievements and sorrows with faithfulness and trust. And, if we are able to emulate these qualities, the lucidity and rich potential of each moment comes into clearer focus. We are stronger and wiser as we follow our soul-directed paths.

The dog is the most faithful of animals and would be much esteemed were it not so common. Our Lord God has made his greatest gifts the commonest.
—Martin Luther, German theologian (1483-1546)

Chapter 1

MYSTICISM AND DOGS

God give me by your grace what you give to dogs by nature.
—Mechtilda of Magdeberg, German hermit and author (1207-1282)

Mysticism is an avenue of life, a way of experiencing reality. Our mystical side is the deepest part of who and what we are. It is the truest part of our nature. It allows us to expand our awareness and understanding; to gain a broader perspective of our existence; to see life in its totality. Mysticism is a great and precious gift that nourishes our soul, our essence. Einstein spoke of it as, "standing rapt in awe." *The Oxford Universal Dictionary* describes the mystic as one who, "seeks by contemplation and self-surrender to obtain union with or absorption into Deity, or who believes in the spiritual apprehension of truths inaccessible to the understanding."

When we open to the mystical state, our dominant mental approach is suspended, allowing our emotions, senses, and instincts to provide us guidance. This quality has been consciously recognized and revered for centuries, generally in individuals who retained the celestial desire of a child playing, frolicking in nature, delighted with each moment.

Mystical activity in Europe throughout the early Christian period occurred primarily during periods of strong intellectual and artistic progress. The advancement of historical mystical figures seemingly burst forth at these times, vitality personified—carrying this wave of progress into the collective spiritual realm.

During the medieval period, Gothic cathedrals were erected, with the arts, religion and philosophy of the period flourishing, including the system of chivalry and the concept of public service. This vital era produced many saints, prominent in the established religious milieu, but few mystics. Perhaps they sought the treasures of growth and spiritual advancement in traditionally less esteemed places—during play or attending to the suffering. Or perhaps they endeavored to establish and pursue extreme challenges—experience failure, or, as is well known, immerse themselves in the soul and substance of nature—in everything vital: discovering God in all things. Hildegard proclaimed, "Every creature is a glittering, glistening mirror of divinity," and, "Every creature is a ray of God."

Fourteenth century Europe was filled with eminent contemplatives who used the academic vigor of the times to increase interest in the profound experiences of the transcendental life. The Renaissance of the sixteenth century explored every aspect of existence and advancement, redefining the world. The successes of each spiritual leader were generally built on the accomplishments and contributions of earlier doyens. They, in turn, enriched the tradition with their own personal interpretations before passing the torch into the future.

Theresa of Avila described this self-knowledge as the "basement" of the soul, if conceived as a structure. Catherine of Siena considered it the "cell" from which the soul grows. The mystic does not take life for granted. Writers in the mystic tradition, both pagan and Christian, held fervently to the belief that God is in all things and that every element of life should be respected and revered.

> *I am the living and fiery Essence of the divine substance that glows in the beauty of the fields. I shine in the water, I burn in the sun, and the stars. Mine is the mysterious force of the*

*invisible wind. I permeate all things, that they may not die. I
am Life.*

—St. Hildegard of Bengen (1098 - 1179)

*Be praised, my Lord, for all your creatures.
In the first place for the blessed Brother Sun,
Who gives us the day and enlightens us through you.
Be praised, my Lord, for Brother Wind
And the airy skies, so cloudy and serene. . .
Be praised, my Lord, for our sister, Mother Earth,
Who nourishes us and watches us
While bringing forth abundance of fruits with colored flowers
And herbs. . .
Be praised, my Lord, for our sister, Bodily Death,
Who no living man can escape.
Praise and bless my Lord.
Render thanks.
Serve God with great humility*

—St. Francis of Assisi (1182- 1226)

And, an early pedagogue who valued the wisdom and contributions of the natural world and the endowments it bestows:

*Apprehend God in all things, for God is in all things. Every
single creature is full of God and is a book about God. Every
creature is a word of God.*

—Meister Eckhart (1260 - 1327)

An early dog lover entreats us to follow their model of loyalty:

*A dog barks when his master is attacked. I would be a cow-
ard if I saw that God's truth is attacked and yet would remain
silent.*

—John Calvin (1509 - 1564)

A more contemporary thinker beseeches us to strengthen our
partnership with the animal world:

> *Hear our humble prayer, O God, for our friends, the animals.*
> *Especially for animals who are suffering; for any that are*
> *hunted or lost or deserted or frightened or hungry; for all*
> *that must be put to death. We entreat for them all thy mercy*
> *and pity. And for those who deal with them, we ask a heart*
> *of compassion, gentle and kindly words. Make us true friends*
> *of the animals and so to share the blessings of the merciful.*
> —Albert Schweitzer

Evelyn Underhill captures the subtle potency of mysticism in her superb tome *Mysticism*. She describes, in detail, how mysticism transforms life (rather than merely contemplating change) as it combines spiritualism (an individual's ability to assimilate and maintain a relationship with God) with a fundamental appreciation of all that is. This activity absolutely influences and dominates the mystic's path, and is inseparable from it. When the mystic and his "path" are one, the dominant life emotion becomes love.[1]

The mystic's purist desire is to give. At times, this process leads to the releasing of everything, including self and illusions, to overcome the confines of our physical and material excesses. The urging that inspires a being to give to such a degree ultimately yields the wisdom that to acquire such self-knowledge is to know all aspects of one's universe.

> *Not only every other human being, but all animals, plants,*
> *stones, everything was one unity, making nonsense of the*
> *view that only human beings have souls. There is no such*
> *thing as time as we know it. Everything that is, has been, is*
> *and always be . . . And we are here and now in eternity.*[2]
> —RERU *1916*

As Underhill describes it, mysticism is, "essentially a movement of the heart, seeking to transcend the limitations of the individual standpoint and to surrender itself to ultimate Reality; for no personal gain; to satisfy no transcendental curiosity; to obtain no other-worldly joys, but purely from an instinct of love."[3] Our personal relationships with animals can assist us on this path to enchantment. We all have the potential to be mystics, to transcend the ordinary, to commit to a place of enormous valor and magnanimity.

Like our canine counterparts, mysticism is active and sensible, focused on a personal object of love, guided by the heart, with no expectation of reward. There are numerous references to animals' relationships with God in the Hebrew Bible. *Rom.* 8:18-23 speaks of their deliverance; *Ps.* 104:27-31, that they abide in God for comfort. *Ps.* 148:7-10 affirms that they will be attendant throughout eternity and *Isa.* 65:25, *Rev.* 5:13-14, that they may be redeemed by God.

> *The mystic takes nothing for granted and shows respect and reverence towards all forms of life. This earth is the honey of all beings; all beings the honey of this earth, the bright eternal Self that lives in this body, are one and the same; that is immortality, that is Spirit, that is all.*[4]
>
> —The Ten Principal Upanishads

For the mystic, love is the ultimate source of joy. As Sophy Burnham describes it, "In fact what the mystic saw was that nothing exists but love: there is no wrong so long as we love."[5] It is the measure of real progress. It is the secret of the universe, the life force of all things.

> *It was granted me to perceive in one instant how all things are seen and contained in God. I did not perceive them in their proper form, and nevertheless the view I had of them was of sovereign clearness, and has remained impressed upon my soul . . . The view was so subtle and delicate that the understanding cannot grasp it.*[6]
>
> —Saint Teresa of Avila

Chapter 2

MYSTICAL MISTER

Mister was a handsome collie-shepherd cross: a forager of adventure, a defender of the vulnerable—wise counselor, steady navigator. And, he was my first love. As a child, raised on the Double Diamond cattle ranch in western Montana, ranch dogs shared my life for as long as memory serves me. My earliest recollections of Mister began when I was around five—old enough to feel awe at the exceptional qualities of this wondrous creature and appreciate what he contributed to my life. He blended perfectly with the earth-spice smells and radiant hues of the ranch. His thick, coarse coat of brown, amber, and black provided a field of comfort for my tears, when I felt sad or exasperated, and a warm haven for my frosted fingers as the north country weather grew colder.

Over the years, our ranch was home to several dogs who, most likely, shared Mister's genetic ancestry. Regardless of the slant or substance of the day, joy, adventure, protection, and exceptional companionship were always assured through the company of our ranch dogs. Work dogs were invariably present on our ranch and all surrounding ranches. Their presence seemed a prerequisite—the sentry, the gatekeeper—or, perhaps, most ranchers have simply developed an acute awareness of what just makes good sense.

The working dogs I remember from my childhood kept watchful vigils over the cattle herds, especially during calving season. They would sound an alert when an unfamiliar presence came within close proximity and provide a watchful eye over every element that entered their domain. At an early age, I came to respect and honor their contributions to my life and to the lives of those I loved. The dominant energy that I sensed from these hearty companions was love, combined with keen interest, staunch protection, and a deep, abiding loyalty. Their affection, and the gentle compassion that they displayed towards my family, and to the other life forms on the ranch, emerged unlimited, unwavering.

Mister and I fashioned a bond, an alliance that transcended mere friendship—we were inseparable. Whatever adventure piqued my interest, Mister was there, without fail, at my side. Most often, he led the way. Coyotes serenaded the countryside as the curtain of dusk descended, and barn owls, white-tail deer, badgers, beaver, weasels, mink, and bears found sustenance and shelter in this lush frontier bottom-land. The surrounding rolling hills, wheaten-hued and arid, rose in huge mounds to the north, providing our ranch house with a solid shield from the prevailing, northerly winds.

To the keen observer, the fertile hay fields, seesaw swaying grasses, dense expanses of cottonwoods and cedar trees, and waters—flowing creeks, and stagnant ponds, each contained and supported countless visages of life, in all their subtle and glorious splendor. And, as an offspring of nature myself, I imbued each waking moment with as many adventures and stirring encounters with these macrocosms of wonders as a young body and soul could summon.

Our ranch was nestled along the meandering Beaver Creek, a mile above its confluence with the Missouri River—the heart of Broadwater County. The ranch encompassed an enchanting blend of meadows, aspen and birch groves, rolling hills and dense, musky stands of ancient evergreen trees. Woodpeckers often selected the stately cottonwood trees as a temporary residence in which to raise their young. The nestlings waited and grew, out of sight and danger, deep within a hollowed tree core. There, they were safe from predators, like the magpies that also occupied the neighborhood. To solidify their niche in nature's hierarchy, magpies, glistening ebony and white scavengers, constructed huge nests, basket-like creations, massive enough to easily shelter a family of eagles. And the scope of the magpie diet excluded very little.

On the edge of the upper meadow lay the charred remains of my great-grandparents' three-story, Victorian home. The structure, barely finished when lightening struck, burned to the ground. Old photos show the beginnings of a yard, as a settled place, separated from the dense, unbroken meadow. But, fifty years later, all that was once new and vital now moldered—scattered in crumbling, weathered shards.

With the advent of summer vacation, our one-room school house, and its routines and responsibilities, were promptly forgotten. Freedom, fresh springtime air, and the promise of new life abounded in every direction. There were adventures to be pursued, imaginations to inspire! Poking through the remaining relics of the old homestead sparked images of a bygone era and provided rich fodder for our childhood play-fantasies. The irregular edge of the foundation wall created a perfect course for balancing contests. And, for my brothers and I (who constantly challenged each other in any area of daring or competence we could conceptualize), this crude gymnastics course dispensed an equitable share of triumphs, dashed hopes, scraped elbows and twisted ankles. Mister oversaw our antics and invariably had a wet kiss for his fallen heroes.

The collapsed icehouse still brimmed with mounds of sawdust and provided the resident mice ample nesting opportunities. Nearby, an ancient barn, weathered to brilliant amber, was filled with pristine horse-drawn farming equipment. It was no longer used and barely remembered, except by my grandfather, Daniel Boone Filson. His ancestors homesteaded in Montana in 1863, and he persevered with their vision.

Since my grandfather lived with us (or we with him), his historical perspective bridged the connections to our predecessors, and helped us envision bygone customs of ranching. Grandpa's ease and appreciation of nature produced a balanced world-view, broad, radiant and kindly respectful. He possessed an intimate familiarity with every detail of the ranch he had created; he merged with the land, his wise and gentle nature a fundamental element—the historian, the originator.

Beaver Creek wound its way though the woods, creating a sparkling, aqueous border around the spacious, open lower meadow. Years of high waters had eroded the earth from the roots of some of the enormous trees, creating small caves; these dark, shrouded worlds, invited our exploration. In addition to their unusual visual allure, these caverns also provided excellent hiding places for mischievous, daring children (and Mister) as we engaged in an earnest game of hide and seek. The dens provided such prime coverage, that, unless the seekers were highly motivated, protection from being discovered was virtually ensured. At times, half an hour or more would pass, and the hiders might wonder if they were still being sought; or had the seekers wandered off in pursuit of another escapade? The delights of these adventures made it matter little, the direction that the events of the day unfolded. There was perpetually some interesting facet of the ranch to explore, and the fertile imagination of youth, combined with Mister's insatiable curiosity, provided any missing or desired elements.

Encounters with rattlesnakes occurred frequently and heightened the drama already unfolding in our recurring adventures. We found snakes everywhere on the ranch: coiled in rocky ledges, moving silently through the tall grasses—bull snakes, garter snakes, rattlesnakes, sometimes in places you would scarcely expect. One sweltering summer afternoon, we watched a rattler wind its way up and over our heads as it navigated through the branches of a scrub tree, overhanging the spring. Snakes overhead—a sobering thought!

From the time we were very young, my brothers and I knew that rattlesnakes usually travel in pairs. As I combed the contours of the ranch, either on horseback or by foot, the drama and trepidation of encountering a rattler was somehow tempered, knowing that Mister also understood about snakes and would engage his senses in finding them, watching for the hidden, inscrutable, second one. Once you learn the ways of the rattler, you understand that you should never consider them with anything but respect; you give them a wide birth; keep your eyes open, and watch your back.

Each spring, Mister kept our cattle herd in order as we migrated on the annual cattle drive, relocating the Herefords to their alpine, summer pasture. Our entire family departed before daybreak, traveling the entire day. We returned at dusk, exhausted and grimy, but satisfied, with memories of this special journey made twice a year. There were endless hazards and challenges—something different each year. But some rituals were consistent. The saddle horses, feeling spirited from lack of exercise throughout the long winter, often displayed their bucking techniques and taxed our patience, even more than usual, at four in the morning. As the drive unfolded, we periodically came upon wounded or dead antelope, impaled on barbed-wire fences as they desperately tried to flee from the reckless and unmindful highway hunters. Even as a child I felt contempt for those thoughtless rogues, too lazy even to leave their vehicles, who found it sporting to target practice on anything that moved.

From a drowsy child's perspective, the scope of this journey seemed vast. When the sun finally broke over the horizon, we became oriented to the foothills we traversed. In this unfamiliar terrain I always pondered, "Was this Kimber Gulch? Did we have the right gulch?" I fantasized that a misjudgment could land us in a sweeping and unknown wilderness. But, regardless of the conditions we encountered, Mister prevailed with a steadfast determination, keeping his priorities in order. With his abiding sense of place and purpose, he never lost a calf or any of his human charges.

Back on the ranch, there were, invariably, chores that required attention. Each day, late in the afternoon, I retrieved our Holstein milk cow, Moe, for her evening milking. Mister provided us both with his ebullient, reliable company. Moe, Mister, and I had such a complete mastery of this routine, that our threesome appeared to be merely going through the motions. But, consistency and routine can engender substance and comfort to life, creating unspoken bonds and abiding trust. And so, we all performed our duties and calmly shared this daily ritual as a stalwart team.

Since Beaver Creek flowed directly past our house, my brothers and I became proficient at fishing early in life. Not that we didn't occasionally impale a hook on an exposed body part. But, for the most part, the equipment was used as it was intended, and the fish were too plentiful not to lure something. At times, landing an empty tin can, tossed into the eddy by a heedless fisherman, was the high point of an afternoon. But, still, those cans put up a good fight and gave us a chance to test the true strength of our lines and fishing prowess.

Mister inspected the brook trout and suckers that we caught, although not as zealously as the barn cats. They were always on the lookout for an easy meal. He was there, primarily, to watch over us. And, while he provided protection, he also shared in our daring adventures. His fascination with the results of our activities showed how intensely he engaged in nature's workings.

As Silver, one of our aging draft horses, struggled with infirmity, finally no longer able to stand, Mister stood guard, chasing away scavengers. He rendered a kindred kindness, a generous mercy, to a young calf suffering from a snake bite. As a silent sentinel, he remained nearby, showing quiet comfort and concern when nothing more could be done. It was as if he had a superior sense of the balance of life, death, and peril, and, in his own serene, knowing manner, found the most appropriate response to the situation: love and companionship.

Throughout our travels, Mister and I traversed every section of the ranch. Some areas held more appeal than others, but every adventure we shared held some memorable enchantment. On one day, we might explore the high drama of skirting the edge of the bullpen. Perhaps the next was spent rescuing an orphaned cottontail bunny from the haying machines and nursing it through the trauma. When the direction seemed unclear, or my nerves felt unsteady, Mister somehow conveyed a sure and safe response. His calm sensibility tempered my youthful fearlessness, and, at the end of the day, we arrived home safely, contented from a day fully lived and, for me, stocked with many lively tales to share.

But Mister taught me that life is more than just an interesting story. Days spent with him were a marvelous introduction to the joys and wonders of friendship: trust, honesty and loyalty. Our love for each other, and our commitment to experiencing joyful escapades, set a standard in my young, impressionistic world—the level by which other relationships would forever be measured.

A seminal part of my youth was spent with a master. Mister was that master—a master of love and truth, fully engaged with Life. He endured, warmly and passionately, and each minute, clear and true, was crystal purity satiated with wholeness. My fine friend gave abundantly and, equally significant, he *received* graciously. He was truly wise, yet he accepted the status quo with humor and playfulness—not brandishing the need to impose his desires onto others in the impudent manner so commonly encountered in human relationships. Mister was strong and gentle and, at the same time, steadfast and flexible as the situation required—perceptive and sagacious on so many levels. I yearned to learn from him—to reach the ancient wisdom he held in his heart. He revealed and I understood, with looks and touch. No need for words.

> *In the field with him, in the autumn, though, as we move*
> *through the light and shadows, I can hear, some days dimly*
> *but other days as if with a shouted roar, some of the silent*
> *fury and joy passing through his blood as he runs — and I*
> *can almost feel it in my own blood.*[1]
>
> —Rick Bass from *Colter*

Chapter 3

APPLE SCRUFFS

Many years would pass and a myriad of life experiences transpire before I would again encounter the wondrous bliss of canine camaraderie. When I was twelve, in the full magnificence of pre-adolescence, our ranch was sold. Our ancestors settled in Broadwater County one hundred years before, during the Civil War era when Montana was still a territory dominated by the fever of the Gold Rush. The ranch was my life-blood. My soul felt crushed, defeated; I could not imagine any other life. The vast meadows, the mysteries of Beaver Creek, the memories I adored that had nurtured me through every facet of childhood, were left behind.

Neighbors and friends, our familiar woods, the spring run-off, and all of my good hiding places, the sweet aromas of the changing seasons, and, most poignant of all, Mister, and all of my beloved animal friends were left, gone—erased from my life, as if they had died. It was deemed that they belonged on the ranch, that they would not adjust to living in town. And, on some deep level, as much as I resisted, I accepted that truth. Occasional visits were agonizing, knowing that, in a few short hours, I would again have to say good-bye. For years my soul raged in silent rebellion at this affront: to what I loved, to adolescent reasoning, and to the harmony that kept my heart at peace.

For six long years I reluctantly participated in a suburban lifestyle. Our house was located just two blocks behind the state capitol building in Helena. Compared to the expansive hayfields and the woods of the ranch, our small yard seemed hardly worth the effort. My lifelong friendships were a thing of the past. None of the junior high cliques, into which I was thrust, had even heard of the small ranch community of Winston, the lost passion of my life. But, there was no going back, and I knew it. My only reasonable hope of escape was into the future and hopefully somewhere far away.

After graduation from high school, I migrated to Missoula and experienced college and the 1970's in unison. The warm acceptance of that community, and the free spirit movement of that era, filled a void within me that had long craved such approval and acceptance.

The challenges and swirling dimensions of academia blended with new-found friendships. Anti-war rallies, rock concerts, road trips to the west coast, scholarships, adventures, and freedom dominated that era. The pain of my loss felt far away. I welcomed a new life.

It was no surprise that I embraced this emancipation, this new found liberty, with the joy and comfort of finding a long-absent friend. By nature, I had always been independent and freedom-loving. I tested the waters and stretched the limits, much as I had during my childhood escapades on the ranch. Once again, the vigor of life fueled my body. My mind was challenged by science and soothed by art. Discovering the potential of self-realization and cultivating the necessary confidence to attempt such daring feats again, guided my path towards true self-discovery.

Although I had many college friends to share these breakthroughs, the solitary journeys that had been such a part of my early childhood often beckoned to me. The quiet act of meditation in nature conveyed a solace to my soul. Silence created a space for inspiration, for the final defining characteristics of emerging young adulthood.

An insistent longing for a calm and abiding companion compelled me to ferret out a friend to share these quiet, yet saturated, moments. My journey towards expanded awareness habitually involved solitary sojourns into the wild back-country, treks in the western wastelands, hikes to alpine lakes, and excursions to the Pacific coast. The minimum requirement to experience the grandeur of these places, the magnificence of the earth's raw energy, was just to physically make the journey—to simply show up. After that, it became a matter of receptivity, immersing in and absorbing the surrounding splendor.

Although I had many soul-satisfying expeditions by myself, it seemed that they would be more absolute and gratifying, if I shared them—not only to witness, with another set of eyes, the resplendent glory, but also to enhance the shelter of the sanctuary. If the weather cooperated and a restless mood came over me, I often departed to the great outdoors in a very spontaneous fashion. It was not uncommon for me to range miles into the woods, alone, and with minimal supplies. And although I have always been blessed with good fortune in these circumstances, the thought of having a trusty companion conveyed a sense of comfort and added security. Specifically, I craved the company of a dog, and, since I was now an adult (barely), this was a decision I could make on my own.

When I contemplated the wide variety of dog breeds, my attention was always drawn to the working breeds. On the ranch, they had provided stability and protection. Their thick coats, hearty dispositions, and calm, sheltering natures lent suitability to my lifestyle. Their playful exuberance and zest for adventure kept pace with my own. So, during my junior year in college, subsisting primarily on brown rice and soup, I welcomed into my life 'Apple Scruffs,' a purebred Old English Sheepdog puppy named after a popular George Harrison song. I called him 'Scruff,' and we started our life together with three roommates, no fenced yard, and a '65 VW Beetle that ran intermittently. Yet, with Scruff in my life, things seemed much closer to perfection than they had in a long time.

Old English Sheepdogs start small and grow rapidly. As a puppy he had a striking black and while coat and patches of pink on his nose. The nose was soon black and his adult coat emerged, a soft downy layer of flowing gray and white wool. Scruff was my constant companion, my confidante, my protector—a clown to clear any leaden moods, and an exuberant comrade to navigate our new course. I had never before had an indoor pup. I soon learned that life with a puppy is an era where you regularly find mangled "remnants" lying about the house and can't help but think, "This was once something useful." But positive identification is impossible; so you toss the remains to avoid undue mental torment and move on.

Because he accompanied me constantly, Scruff developed a pure and dependable social presence with people and animals alike. He became a peer within my circle of friends, and I sensed that others, too, found his demeanor comforting. He was solid and honest, and steadfastly guided others in that direction.

Throughout my college years and my burgeoning young adulthood, Scruff was my foremost and constant friend. He had a lumbering, good-natured, accepting personality. He seemed to enjoy everyone, and consistently treated other animals with open regard. One of my roommates, Margie, shared her life with a large, orange tomcat named Chuck. Scruff and Chuck were the household mascots and were genuinely fond of each other. Chuck was portly built and often suffered from abscesses, the result of numerous tomcat skirmishes. This medical condition slowed him down and weakened his ability to defend himself.

One day, we heard the roweling begin—another confrontation taking shape. Scruff was instantly out the door, a flashing streak of gray and white hair, heading for the back yard. He swept past me on his way to intercept the fight, one eye peeking through his white mop of hair. Chuck was arched and bristled, ready (at least in his mind) for yet another whirling tempest. The two opponents torpidly circled each other, sizing up the situation. Scruff slid to a stop and merely stood near

Chuck, gazing at the challenger. Scruff, by presenting a Sheepdog shield, provided Chuck his support—passive, yet potent. The other cat contemplated Scruff's massive bulk, and, sensing the tables had turned, simply walked away. The entire incident ended with no violence— Scruff's version of providing protection and re-establishing harmony.

Intimacy and true concern shaped Scruff's demeanor, his legacy. With the ability to distill the complexities of life into an enduring simplicity, he persevered for the weak and elevated their hopes. His coded heritage held a strong do-or-die optimism, his domain an abiding compilation of trust and wariness. Touch-and-go, on the edge of an abyss—the protector, waiting to discern the answer.

Two months following my graduation from college, I accepted my first job as a social worker in Deer Lodge, a small town in rural Montana, and moved into a tiny house in the country, about three miles from town. It was an old, run-down, ranch-hand quarters, heated entirely with wood— complete with a contaminated well and a resident pack rat. Could this be our home? Peeling, pocked walls were all that separated us from the fields and the errant, straying cattle and coyotes. Crowns of sage surrounded us, and a mountain of firewood provided warmth, in spite of the frigid, leaking frame. For all the uncertainty, there was no loneliness, just a full burst of creation vibrating within our hearts—received with a haunting urgency. We were on our own, and the rent was great. Fifty bucks a month and plenty of solitude!

My office was in the basement of the original courthouse and had a window overlooking the front lawn. Every morning, I bid Scruff adieu and made my way to town, by car or bicycle, depending on the weather. Scruff had never been to my office. He seemed content to stay at the house, protecting the home front and keeping the cats, Prissy, Emma Lou, and Simon company. One morning I glanced up to find Scruff curled in front of my office window, gazing in. It seemed he needed his own confirmation of my whereabouts, and perhaps, of my safety.

Deer Lodge is home to the Montana state prison, and our rustic residence was located directly on one of the main escape routes, a facile avenue into the isolated Boulder hills. One dim, blustery winter night, Scruff began barking fiercely outside, behavior very unusual for this calm guardian. Suddenly, I heard a man's voice yell, "Shut up!" directly outside the bathroom window. Without Scruff and his dependable instincts, I would have felt truly isolated and vulnerable. But, somehow I summoned some courage and felt the need to lend support to my salient ally. I retrieved the .22 rifle my brother, Tom, had given me for such occasions, inserted the clip and stepped outside the backdoor. I fired a couple of rounds into the air. Shortly, all was quiet. I brought Scruff inside, locked the door, and pondered the veracity of our situation. Maybe fifty bucks was not such a bargain after all.

One summer, for a diversion, I resurrected an ancient, crusty pickup truck from a local rancher's field. This primitive driving machine, a 1951 half ton GMC with significant dents, sported a royal blue paint job, generously applied (or so it appeared) with a whisk broom. The original cream color emerged more each year, yielding a wild, striped, exotic look. This old Gimmy was the only vehicle I have ever encountered that had a positive ground electrical system.

The floorboards had long since rusted away, but the engine was strong, and this aged, battered beast was Scruff's delight. How he thrilled to leap into the box, position himself behind the cab, and steady himself for whatever quest lay ahead. The words, "Let's go for a ride," brought such joy to his face, I felt guilty on the occasions when he could not go along.

I kept that ancient truck for almost twenty years. It served many purposes, both recreational and utilitarian, but none more meaningful than the joy it gave Scruff when we loaded up and departed for one of his rapture-filled rides.

After two years, and the acquisition of a stomach ulcer, I resigned my job and pondered my future. My friend, Sara, offered to let us stay in the cabin that her family had built a generation before on Rock Creek Lake, west of Deer Lodge. In that remote setting, we had even more solitude as winter provided a calm backdrop for contemplation. The fireplace provided both heat and light, simple and pure requisites for our survival. But our ultimate departure to civilization was postponed by one storm too many. Gusts from a blizzard buried the vehicles and necessitated a five mile descent on foot, through two feet of fresh snow. It was our only way out.

Later that winter, with pivotal assistance from my brothers, Bill and Tom, I constructed a camper for the old truck. When it was finished and fitted on the truck box with a forklift, I hitched my VW bug to the rear bumper with a home-made tow bar, loaded up Scruff and my essential belongings, and headed for Santa Fe, New Mexico, with our black cat crony, Hattie.

During our first night on the road, the January mercury dipped to minus twenty eight degrees. I roused myself several times during the night and started the sluggish engine to ensure that it would fire up in the morning. The truck was archaic—no sense pushing our luck. But, we were young, in heart and spirit, and each day brought new lessons to test our wits and strengthen our resilience. Towing a vehicle behind an antediluvian, two-wheel drive truck, on black ice, through high winds can be viewed as either a thrilling adventure or insanity, depending on your perspective. And providing you live to tell about! Incredulous on-lookers thankfully kept their sentiments and gestures to themselves, and on we went. The ascent up Raton pass was a creeping affair, ground out in first gear. But I knew that if we ever stopped, we would never get started again. This was not an advisable place to spend the winter, so onward we churned, dwarfed by the snow drifts piled high on both sides, hoping to make it to the top before dark. If the speedometer was accurate, we were averaging five miles per hour. Finally, after what seemed an eternity, we crested the pass and slowly, sluggishly, the engine's rpm's justified a shift to second gear. At last, a different sound for our ears! Scruff was never tolerant of slow travel. He often prompted sluggish drivers with an emphatic round of his ringing barks, delivered out the side window. But, on this pivotal occasion, he stifled his commentary, and kept his opinion to himself.

Scruff, Hattie, and I secured a base of operation in a rugged lean-to on private land with a majestic view that overlooked the valley south of Taos, New Mexico. Dia, the owner, generously offered this remote sanctuary, grateful for another neighbor in this vast, untamed expanse. Her two-story house was constructed of logs that she had skidded down the hill, with only the pulling power of a single horse. Each morning, I split wood for the campfire, brewed tea, and then loaded Scruff into the car, eager to explore northern New Mexico. Spirit opened us to a new rapture in an ancient land, like a strong, primeval drumbeat.

Twenty five years later, I re-created this journey, but this time in the summer, traveling alone in a modern Toyota, four-wheel drive pickup. I could sense Scruff's presence, his abiding spirit by my side— the energy and the joy he always emanated when we traveled together. In the Gimmy, we rarely approached the posted speed limit. But on this journey, we actually kept pace with the traffic. For a thousand miles, the memories of our first trip to New Mexico, punctuated with tears, triggered a remembrance, a tribute to a time when we were both young and vital. As I recalled the many milestones we encountered along the way, I envisioned Scruff, intent on the road ahead, thrilled with the speed.

One of the most powerful and noble qualities of the dog is their ability to live fully in the moment, to respond honestly and directly. To brave life with them, side by side, enriches our lives as we stride down the mystic trail. In their dance with us, dogs merge with us; the watcher and the dancer become one. They can love us undividedly, without completely understanding us. They are attuned to our uncommon aspects, which are unnoticed by the rest of the world.

Scruff and I continued to share many touching moments and exhilarating capers over the years, combined with as many truck rides as possible. After several years, we relocated to the Flathead valley in northern Montana, and Scruff, for the second time (that I know of), became a father. The puppies were beautiful, and, in compensation for the stud service, I kept a pup. I chose a female—a calm, exquisite creature who would sustain Scruff's legacy. Her name was Cuyamungue, "Cuya" for short.

Our threesome shared a chalet on thirty acres, near the south shore of Flathead Lake, where I boarded two horses to keep the pasture grazed. Every evening after work we either went for a ski, took the horses for a romp, or hiked to a nearby hilltop for a view of the Mission Mountain valley—the gateway to Glacier Park. Life was bliss. Scruff shared his time with his divine daughter and, engrossed in my job, I developed new friendships. After years on the road, we all felt contented to settle in the full benevolence of the rural western Montana landscape that surrounded us.

But, as often happens in life, the vivacity of our stable, compact family was cut short. Cuya was barely a year old when Scruff developed lumps along his spine. He tired easily; walks were endured, not enjoyed. Finally, the vet gave the diagnosis: cancer. The particular form of cancer was aggressive and advanced. The vet recommended euthanasia. The devastating reality of saying good-bye to my compatriot of all those year was unbearable. Why was this happening? Scruff was only nine years old.

A friend wrote this song as a gift to me, and a tribute to my beloved Scruff:

We've come so far, together we've seen it;
The day, the nights, forever I'll keep it;
The sun, your soul, so warm while the wind blows;
It's hard, it hurts, the end of a rainbow.

> *It rains, it snows, the seasons are changing;*
> *My dog, he glows, he's Scruff and I'm praying;*
> *The time has come, realizing it's over;*
> *He's happy, he's loved, he knows and he shows her.*

With life they played, ran through the springtime;
With love they made memories for a lifetime;
His face, his eyes, now so shiny and tender;
His bark, his sounds, sounds she'll remember.

We've come so far, together we've seen it;
The days, the nights, forever we'll keep it.
It rains, it snows, the seasons are changing;
My dog, I love you, he's Scruff and I'm praying.

Through the trees he runs, wiping his hair back;
Wide opening his eyes so he can see that
Dorothy, she's here, still running by his side;
Hop in, let's go, we're going for a long ride.[1]

—David Wigton

I buried my dear friend on the top of a high slope overlooking the Flathead River. There, I trusted, his spirit could feel the breezes coming off the river, just as the drafts had cooled him during his many delight-filled truck excursions. I paused, remembering the joy and comfort he brought to my life: from the early days of his puppyhood; during my college years; through my first job, and the many moves we made throughout the West. He was always there for me, calm and assured, wise to the world. He was my guide, my friend, and my shield. As my heart broke and my stomach churned, stifled from this profound loss, Scruff's spirit went home, all suffering behind him—lifted on the wings of love.

The bond with a true dog is as lasting as the ties of this earth
can ever be.

—Konrad A. Lorenz, Austrian naturalist (1903-1989)

If a blade of grass has the power to move you, if the simple
things of nature have a message that you understand, rejoice,
for your soul is alive.

—Eleonora Duse, Italian actress (1858-1924)

Chapter 4

LOVE

I came across a photograph of him not long ago, his black face with the long snout sniffing at something in the air, his tail straight and pointing, his eyes flashing in some momentary excitement. Looking at a faded photograph taken more than forty years before, even as a grown man, I would admit I still missed him.[1]

—Willie Morris from *My Dog Skip*

Love is patient and kind; love is not jealous or boastful; it is not arrogant or rude. Love does not insist on its own way; it is not irritable or resentful; it does not rejoice at wrong, but rejoices in the right. Love bears all things, believes all things, hopes all things, endures all things.

—from Paul's *First Letter to the Corinthians*

Love is, without much uncertainty, the most significant, influential force in our daily lives. We instinctively move towards it and actively seek to increase it in our lives. The lack of love creates a sense of separation which diminishes our self esteem and damages our mental, emotional, and spiritual well being.

Love is a force that feeds our soul at the most fundamental and life-affirming level. Love is real. It is powerful. It is necessary for healthy growth. Young children have been known to die without it. We need love for every level of growth. It connects us with every aspect of our being and brings us ever closer to our higher self.

When we tap into the life-giving Universal flow of love, we begin to notice it in many realms: like-minded people who offer affirmations, the adoration of our pets, the wonders of nature that sustain and nurture us. We come to understand how love can work in our lives, and thus, we seek to multiply this remarkable treasure.

Williams Law's expanded view of love transcends the moment, the standing in relation to others—the species.

> *This is the ground and original of the spirit of love in the creature: it is, and must be, a will to all goodness; and you have not the spirit of love until you have this will to all goodness, at all times, and on all occasions.*

> *You may indeed do many works of love, and delight in them, especially at such times as they are not inconvenient to you, or contradictory to your state, or temper, or occurrences in life, until you live freely, willingly, and universally, according to it . . .*

> *As the sparks know no motion but that of flying upwards, whether it be in the darkness of the night, or in the light of day; so the spirit of love is always in the same course; it knows no difference of time, place or persons; but whether it gives or forgives, bears or forbears, it is equally doing its own delightful work, equally blessed from itself. For the spirit of love, wherever it is, is its own blessing and happiness, because it is the truth and reality of God in the soul.[2]*
>
> —Selected Mystical Writings

Through a state of awareness, it is feasible to discover love all around us. There are infinite opportunities to give and receive love. Can you remember times when you felt loved and longed to duplicate the experience? To help us accomplish this, dogs can be our constant and constructive guides. They help us to face our fears about love: possible rejection, feelings of unworthiness—concern that if we do create love in our lives, we will eventually lose it, and so on.

Dogs play a vital role in the lives of millions of Americans. It is estimated that over 50 million dogs inhabit American homes. We sustain the canine members of our families by purchasing their health care, supplies, doggie day-care, designer dog beds, clothing, shrinks, poochie Prozac—visiting dog web sites, and supporting dog-friendly hotels. For the millions who have experienced dog love, they know that this is a fair exchange to assure the health, comfort and companionship of their best friends. Dogs radiate friendliness and joy towards us, in both good times and bad. When we celebrate or are sick or grieving, we find compassion, that is not transitory or shallow, but solid and steadfast.

Dogs introduce us to a fresh and secure arena where we are free to practice the reciprocation of giving and receiving love. They help us to enjoy love often, in each day, and make it a part of who we are— what we know to be true and present—what we desire to manifest into our lives. By sharing this remarkable benefaction, we discover that our fears and worries are not true reality, but have only the power we grant them. Countless individuals have spent hundreds of hours in therapy, hoping to achieve this realization. But, by directly experiencing the giving and receiving of love, the myths that created our anxious perspectives are shattered. We can release these burdens of dread and distrust.

When we are freed from the expectation to behave in a certain way, under certain conditions, our souls can feast on the endless subtleties and possibilities. The presence of the 'pure' allows us to dive deeply, to see through the shadowed, and make sense of the exhilaration. Catch it if you dare; fill your cup with grace—it will serve you throughout your life.

Author and psychologist, Mary Lou Randour, knows the psychological importance of relationships, "and the paradox that the self only exists through relationships with others. The person we know as 'self' only comes into being through intimate relationships."[3]

For many individuals, the bonds with their pets represent the closest, most reliable relationships in their lives. We know that the trust we place in these animal guardians will not betray us, but will grow and flourish throughout the course of the friendship. We accept the essence of each other with admiration and gratitude, realizing how very little actually separates us.

Author and veterinarian, Allen M. Schoen, has discovered that co-species connections can be mystical and illuminating, "They put us in touch with bonds that modern civilization has forgotten . . . they allow humans and animals alike the chance to develop into something greater than each could be alone."[4]

Dogs possess a total absorption in living. They dwell in, and embrace this glorious world, enticing us to join them in their complete and genuine relationship with love. They will their love to us, even under the most difficult conditions. Dogs project the same loving qualities we see in children—rapt attention to the details of life, filled with wonder and innocence. Their invitation to accept this perennial fountain of unconditional positive regard is ever present, and this in turn fosters our emotional growth.

Dog love makes us feel important. We know where we stand with them. These basic, but important, qualities go a long way towards establishing our security, but are, quite often, lacking in many of our relationships with other people. Dogs, virtually always, return our affection in a passionate, affirming manner. And, if we do not offer them love first, dogs are more than willing to make the first gesture, taking the initiative to generate this magical, healing exchange. Our dog friends are predictable, familiar and supportive—they possess the very characteristics we may wish were more abundant in our human friends and family. They ask naught as they offer a catalyst to a larger experience.

Czech Milan Kundera's character, Teresa, found solace in the company her dog, Karenin, contrasting the torment she experienced from her unfaithful lover.

> *It is a completely selfless love: Tereza did not want anything of Karenin; she did not ever ask him to love her back. Nor had she asked herself the questions that plague human couples: Does he love me? Does he love anyone more that me? Does he love me more than I love him?...*

> *Teresa accepted Karenin for what he was; she did not try to make him over in her image; she agreed from the outset with his dog's love, did not wish to deprive him of it, did not envy him his secret intrigues ...*

> *No one forced her to love Karenin; love for dogs is voluntary.*[5]

It is so natural for us to love dogs, that we touch this feeling effortlessly, although it may be difficult for us to achieve this ease of devotion in another context. In their accepting and non-threatening manner, dogs draw from us our own sense of love, and, in doing so, help heal our emotional wounds as well. Once we experience such unconscious, reflective love, we begin to recognize goodness in all things—the potential for it in all experiences—lying in the sun, returning the smile from a child, the murmur of a breeze through the trees, or sipping cool, crystalline water. Inhaling aromas, the bouquet of springtime, the musk of autumn.

A dog's expression of love is direct, responsive, and absolute. And, in this way, they transcend the limitations, barriers and anxieties so commonplace in the human experience. They connect with something infinite and affirming. In some traditions, it is believed that to attain this connection with this inner experience is to discover our highest Self.

Canine demonstrations of love are spontaneous, open, freely given, and offered in abundance. Dundee, my youngest Westie puppy, loves to share his squeaky toy. He retrieves it from one of his secret hiding places, and entices a companion into a game of tug-of-war, his rump in the air, tail swishing—delight in his eyes. This connection with the object of his love is innocent and pure; it is also very genuine. His devotion promotes a sense of safety and trust in both the giver and receiver. This perfect state of dog-love eases our fears, as we join with something so much greater—so genuine, something far beyond us—something infinite.

The love we receive from dogs opens us to a field of vast possibilities. As we learn to reveal our most tender feelings of vulnerability, the sensation may be accompanied by a deep, sacred sense of boundless joy. Our cheerful, canine friends work their gentle magic. And because of their enduring and steadfast devotion, we can open our hearts, achieving wondrous results—releasing the pain of a lifetime: grief, lack of love, the inability to trust.

Trust overcomes the human ego's need for separateness and self-absorption. Dogs can help us discover the simple pleasures of living. They adore our attention—when we speak to them—the tenderness of a touch. And, as these simple pleasures are reciprocated, our mutual bonds deepen. We need each other, and love each other, plain and simple.

Dogs help us to achieve the confidence to express our best, our truest self, in a natural, instinctive manner—through a comforting exchange of energy and unbounded respect.

Their highly evolved sense of love, loyalty, and devotion inspire us to reach higher in these arenas of our lives as well. These "angels with fur" show us a fresh and vastly more satisfying approach to life through their wise and loving actions. Dogs' innate abilities to love and serve allow them to act as beacons and guides on our journey towards the advancement of our souls. They conduct themselves in such a loving, loyal manner, that many dog lovers believe that it is we humans who are blessed to share their presence. As Mike del Ross of *Guide Dogs for the Blind* said, "Dogs never lie about love."[6]

As devotees of the mystic path, dogs love unconditionally. Regardless of how they are treated, they exude enthusiasm: wanting to be with us, to please us, ever willing to forgive. They help us contact our own inner joy, and help heal both our physical and emotional wounds. The degree to which we achieve happiness can be a telling measure of the success of our living. In essence, this joyful state brings us ever closer to achieving the nature of the Divine.

Dogs, as embodiments of love, loyalty and service (and their perseverance is these realms) sanction the path to becoming whole. By their example in these areas of life, they illuminate the path towards actualization for the rest of us. This advancement is key to our soul evolution, and dogs can be our loving guides throughout this journey. As we venture through this passage, we acknowledge who and what we are, clarifying and defining our hopes and aspirations for the future. Self-confidence evolves from *being* loved which, in turn, helps us *engender* self-love. This inner affirmation propagates a magnanimous openness; we generate the ability to forgive. As we become more accepting of ourselves, we feel more comfortable including others in our lives. And thus, the process unfolds. This self-love motivates us to love and support others as they, too, endeavor to discover their deepest truths.

When we learn to accept and trust ourselves, to clarify our vision and purpose, ideally, we consolidate it with action. We develop the capacity to extend and accept love; we expand in a way that is of paramount importance to the completion of the growth cycle.

If love is offered, there must be someone or some thing willing to receive it. If a recipient for that love is unavailable, it thwarts the ability of the giver to **give**. We benefit the evolution of our own species, and that of other species, by receiving as well as giving love. For the preservation and transformation of earth and all her life-forms, it is essential that this aspiration be given precedence.

> *One last word of farewell, dear master and mistress.*
> *Whenever you visit my grave, say to yourselves with regret*
> *but also with happiness in your hearts at the remembrance of*
> *my long, happy life with you: "Here lies one who loves us*
> *and whom we loved." No matter how deep my sleep I shall*
> *hear you, and not all the power of death can keep my spirit*
> *from wagging a grateful tail.*

[From the last will and testament of Blemie O'Neill, the author's beloved dalmatian.]

—Eugene O'Neill, playwright (1888-1953)

Chapter 5

JOY

I could never quite take dogs for granted. Why were they so devoted to the human race? Why should they delight in our company and welcome us home in transports of joy? Why should their greatest pleasure lie in being with us in our homes and wherever we were? They were just animals after all and it seemed to me that their main preoccupation ought to be in seeking food and protection; instead they dispensed a flow of affection and loyalty which appeared to be limitless.[1]

—James Herriot

When we experience a joyful moment, drink in and savor its succor, we draw more of this majestic bliss into our lives. We manifest what we focus on. Experiencing joy satiates the soul on such a deep and inherently fulfilling level that we relish it—like savoring our favorite meal after a rigorous day hike. Joy sustains us. Our joyful memories provide texture and renewal, a meaning to life that enables us to endure the low points, the challenges that shake us to our core. And, witnessing joy on the faces of those we love provides a satisfaction with life that helps us visualize that a higher level is attainable. Why should we not inhabit that stage on a regular basis?

Sofie discovered this pleasure early in her puppy hood and activated it throughout her life. She originated such abundant joy in her world; it seemed as if she were a physical incarnation of happiness. We have seen it time and again; dogs don't need the presence of certain qualifying conditions to experience joy. They find it all around them; they create happy moments, if they do not presently exist. They resonate with an energy greater than themselves, and congeal this sense of rightness to the greater world. Dogs are willing to take risks, to open their hearts, and flourish from their experiences. They exude a positive energy which others cannot derail and remain true to their path (and pack), seeking what they require to thrive and be content.

In honoring his beloved dog, Chinook, Gary Kowalski tells us, "My dog has deep knowledge to impart. He makes friends easily and doesn't hold a grudge. He enjoys simple pleasures and takes each day as it comes. Like a true Zen master, he eats when he's hungry and sleeps when he's tired. He's not hung up about sex. Best of all, he befriends me with an unconditional love that humans would do well to emulate."[2] Dogs manage to find true contentment with less ego, striving for unconscious delights, whatever their circumstances.

Sophy Burnham encountered this blissful joy when she interviewed the Dalai Lama. She discovered that he could scarcely put two sentences together without bursting into laughter. "Enlightenment brings joy. Anyone who has been in the presence of a highly evolved or holy person has seen this. Moreover, you pick it up from him or her, as if the vibrating particles of that person's energy field excite your own and set them dancing in conjunction with his . . . The enlightened ones, those whom we call saints cannot help but shine and laugh."[3]

Matthew Fox and Rupert Sheldrake, in their collaborative book *Natural Grace*, agree that one of the reasons that our culture is so short on joy is that we're short on grace. They suggest that we need to develop an awareness of being in grace, to discover it in everything, in every moment.

I've never thought of them as synonyms, but I see that you could hardly be joyful without being in a state of grace of some kind. Probably they're closely related.[4]

Dogs abide with the expectation that life can be joyful; they create that reality through new revelations—doggie discoveries that become delightful events. Out of "bad" experiences, dogs learn the necessary lessons, and thus, avoid future, similar occurrences. This stabilizes their balance and harmony, their sense of permanence. And, their openness draws to them, miraculous and life-affirming vigor. When we endeavor to emulate their courage, to embrace the new, the mysterious, we increase our own sensation of aliveness and elevate our sense of adventure. We feel invigorated, more in touch with our childhood sense of wonder and anticipation. To affect new adventures energizes our evolution. We are meant to live replete lives; it is up to us to make the choice for joy, and take a great leap forward towards a contented hereafter. Dogs' joy for life is irrepressible and radiant. It permeates and dominates their nature and their relations to the world around them.

Serving as a surrogate mother to Sofie, in her early development, I endeavored to enhance her experience of the world as a safe place. As she matured, she grew more confident, expressing her joy by enticing and captivating much larger dogs and people she did not know. On our routine hikes, she would crouch on the trails, pretending to stalk these massive dogs as they approached. Little Sofie emulated a small white lioness; her stealth was intense, and her wiggling rear-end provided a critical sense of timing on which she based her impending pounce. Then, at the moment she deemed most fitting, she would fearlessly bound towards the advancing dogs at full speed and jump up on them in an attempt to engage them in play. To my knowledge, none ever rebuffed her roughly, but she certainly placed herself at that risk. Most often, these potential, spontaneous play partners recognized her cues, delighted at her initiative, and joined in her frisky antics.

Their human companions, watching the scene unfold, found these encounters both amusing and endearing. Sofie would then switch her kind attention to the human hikers to convey that she, also, appreciated their presence in her world. With licks and animated tail-wagging, she had the delighted approach to life that one sees in a happy child. She would then continue down the trail; the small pistons of her hindquarters powered her along, as she glided in her own small mist of dust.

In *The Common Experience*, J. M. Cohen and J. F. Phipps herald this propensity for innocence, "Most of our contemporary hucksters at the path's entrance proclaim the uselessness of intellectual effort, the need to be as a little child. But the efforts demanded in order to regain this lost simplicity are frequently considerable."[5] Sofie's undivided approach to her surroundings conveyed impeccable *involvement*, that of a self-actualized, engaged, and joyful spirit, determined to enjoy life as much as possible and do what she could to help those around her discover this happy space as well.

Wolf behaviorists have identified specific actions also found in dogs that demonstrate their pleasure with the world. Jeffrey Masson's dog, Simi, squeals, licks, rolls over, and wags her tail throughout her happiness demonstration. As many dog lovers have witnessed, tail wagging begins early in puppyhood, and endures through the life span of a dog. "It has no function other than a social one, and in all these respects is much like the human smile."[6]

In *Animal Grace* Mary Lou Randour characterizes this type of "innocence" in children as unspoiled wisdom: "Children are untainted by cultural prejudice that dismisses or demeans the position of animals in our lives. To children, animals are not lower—they are fellow beings of equal standing, worthy of the same treatment as a fellow human . . . It is the very realness of animals, a realness paradoxically brought to life through how they differ from our human species, that contrasts with the virtual reality of the computer games and videos that inundate children's lives."[7]

Jeffrey Masson believes that dogs, like children, feel happiest and most content in places that contain pleasant memories for them. For many dogs, this involves being engulfed in the spirit and elements of the outdoors—the smells of a marsh, by the sight of wild flowers coming up in the grass fields.

> *The feeling world of dogs is suffused with innocence, purity, and lack of self-deception, something that dogs have in common with children. Both children and dogs have a certain openness, a lack of guile, and also a similar vulnerability. Dogs remind us of our children. We have the same irresistible urge to use baby talk with both. We give them nicknames; we use facial expressions that make people without children or dogs think we're demented.*[8]

Dogs enjoy teasing each other, and being kindly teased by humans. Dogs tease back, using expressions that indicate they are getting away with something. Small or disabled dogs instinctively adapt so their unique characteristics do not prevent them from living the most complete, joyous life possible. Sofie was true to herself, risking all consequences, including physical danger, to achieve her mission. She brought to each life situation her own unique wholesomeness and shared it with the world. She related to her environment with intense interest, enthusiasm and regard. This wonderment and joy delighted and expanded her as she cast her mystical spell on the world around her. Her life experience was rich with simple joys, pleasures, and adventures. On our hikes near Bozeman, up the nearby Sourdough drainage, Sofie could scarcely contain herself until we reached a deep, calm pool created above an enormous beaver dam. There, she would contentedly swim laps, soaking all but the crown of her small white head, luxuriating in the coolness that would make the rest of her hike more pleasurable.

Sofie required very little to be happy. In fact, she seemed to manifest happiness from the core of her being. She was at ease with herself and the world around her. Momentary setbacks, such as being stepped on by Sadie, her Old English sheepdog "sister," who outweighed her by 80 pounds, brought only a transitory expression of hurt and displeasure. Soon her innate capacity to forgive and rebound took over, and she resumed her delightful participation in the grand adventure of her life.

In facing her own diagnosis of cancer, author Susan Chernak McElroy internalized the belief that the solution to overcoming fear is to exercise delight in the present. Her beloved dog, Keesha, who had died years earlier from cancer, provided her with the inspiration to face her own fate, whatever it might be. She remembered that, up until her final moments, Keesha managed to find joy in each day; that the antidote to fear is to practice joy in the moment.

> *Several weeks before her death, Keesha had become quite weak from her disease. The long daily strolls along the marsh near our home became shorter and shorter as her cancer spread. In her healthier days, Keesha's greatest joy had been to swim in the deep lagoons filled with cattails and marsh grass. But now, too frail to swim, she looked to the glossy, shallow pools of rain that peppered our streets. At every opportunity, Keesha would plop into a big puddle and splash and bark for as long as I'd let her. The look on her face during those times was the look of a hog in a wallow. On our last excursion together she was only days away from death, yet she was in bliss . . . at joy Keesha was a master.[9]*

In 1930, an unknown photographer captured a heart-wrenching image of Shep, a two-legged dog who walked only on his hind legs. An accompanying clip tells how Shep, who lived with a family named Rattigan, saved his life by chewing off both front legs when he was caught in a wolf trap. He taught himself to walk upright and got along quite well. Apparently the Humane Society believed he should be shot, but the Rattigans refused. They regarded Shep as family and were even more attached to him in view of his courage and spunk. The photo shows Shep, with a joyful look on his face, tongue out, posing with his human guardian.[10] If Shep could endure and overcome such a life threatening trauma, and still face life with a joyful attitude, perhaps there is a lesson here for the rest of us.

Our modern, high-tech lifestyles, which preclude much interaction with the natural world, enhance, even more, the appreciation many of us have for the pets in our lives. It is possible that they remind us of our own ancient roots, when our ancestors were engaged in a deeper, more dynamic, natural life experience. Dogs are masters at playing, expressing pleasure, and forming spontaneous, loving relationships. By observing and modeling them, they can teach us to confront our fears: to perceive that the world is safe; that we never lose, even though we are in a constant state of change.

As Tereza discovered about her dog, Karenen, she positively enjoyed being welcomed into the day by him. "Waking up was sheer delight for him; he always showed a naive and simple amazement at the discovery that he was back on earth; he was sincerely pleased."[11]

Dogs delight in displaying the miraculous exchange of play. They even have a specific signal to engage each other in this marvelous pastime, the play bow. When encountering another dog, they drop their forelegs to the ground, stare into their potential playmate's eyes, and wag their tails. Ordinarily, when a dog looks another dog directly in the eye, it is seen as a challenge. But, the play bow is universally accepted for what it is intended, an invitation to frolic. It is an important reminder to not take life too seriously. Make time and room in your life for play and joy. Create your own "play bow" and use if often!

Animal rights activist, Roger Caras, tells of how one of his most remarkable dog companions, Sirius, a retired racing greyhound, came to join their family. Each year, hundreds of these race dogs are put to death because homes cannot be found for them. One day a rescue committee went to a track in New Hampshire knowing that they had only three openings. They were low in spirits because they already had more dogs than potential homes. On that particular day, they were presented with twenty-five lovely dogs, all less than four years old, and many under three. They quickly chose three and left sadly, knowing the other twenty-two would die later that afternoon.

Sirius was one of those not chosen, simply because there was not room. He was a beautiful, healthy dog, and he also had an unusual habit of "smiling", rolling his lips back to show his teeth. He did this on many occasions: when greeting someone, when he was about to get a cookie, or when he was asked (to smile). It was simply his way of interacting with people. In wolf packs, it is how a socially superior animal is acknowledged.

That afternoon, one of the rescue committee members received a message from the veterinarian whose task it was to put the dogs to sleep. She called the veterinarian who said: "Look, I've killed twenty-one healthy young dogs this afternoon, but I am not going to do this big white-and-brown male in. How do you kill a dog that smiles at you every time you come near him with a syringe?"

And that is how Sirius came to join the Caras family on their farm. Roger went to Maryland to do a television report on the tragic fate of track greyhounds. Sirius walked over to him, looked into his face and smiled. How could he say no?[12]

> *A dog wags its tail with its heart.*
> —Martin Buxbaum, writer (1919-1991)

> *With eyes upraised, his master's look to scan,*
> *The joy, the solace, and the aid of man;*
> *The rich man's guardian, and the poor man's friend,*
> *The only creature faithful to the end.*
> —George Crabbe

Chapter 6

CONTEMPLATION AND ACTION

*We learn then to be at home in the dark and in the light, in
suffering and in joy, in riches and in poverty. We learn surprises and openness to the spirit. We learn stillness and the
silence that is behind all things. We learn to be with awe and
to let it fill us.*[1]

—Matthew Fox

*Animals, in their blessed state of total presence, require our
presence as well. All animals possess the enviable quality of
complete acceptance of the moment—a quality some of us
meditate on for a lifetime, only to achieve in small measure.
Coming into animal presence, we may find ourselves refresh-
ingly alert to living in the moment.*[2]

—Susan Chernak McElroy

Dog-days contain expansive periods of time spent in silent
observation of their surroundings, immersed in the ebb and flow of
nature. In response, dogs incorporate into their beings the calming,
healing effects of nature, and, in turn, pass on that sense of completion
and renewal of their source to those around them. By interacting with
nature, and affirming their place in the grand design of life, dogs reach
a state of deep peace; they come to terms with what they are and where
they fit in the interrelation of all things. Dogs possess the mystical

capacities to be both active and passive as they practice the direct, immediate experience of reality. They live in a state of devotion to those they love and look with eyes of constancy. They can be still in tranquility and truly *immerse* in a state of affinity.

Spending such extended intervals in meditation might seem excessive. What could *possibly* be gained from such an activity? Perhaps that is the ultimate lesson—the purpose is not to gain, but to be. The Dalai Lama meditates for four hours a day and considers himself to be a novice. Mother Theresa prayed for four hours a day and firmly believed she could not do her work without that time of renewal.[3]

To do, or not to do. Sadie, the sheepdog, and the young Westies, Scotia and Dundee, spend a great deal of time outdoors, where the yard provides them with infinite choices. The resident squirrels and cottontail rabbits definitely pique their interest. A hot summer day might divert them to a dip in the creek or a cool respite under the blue spruce. As one season fades into the next, morning into afternoon, perhaps a nap might do. Whatever is fitting to the situation, their clear intuition provides direction, and they respond with natural and instinctive enthusiasm.

In *Mysticism*, Evelyn Underhill relates, "In mysticism that love of truth which we saw as the beginning of all philosophy leaves the merely intellectual sphere, and takes on the assured aspect of a personal passion . . . the mystic lives and looks; and speaks, consequently, the disconcerting language of first-hand experience . . . the Absolute of the mystics is lovable, attainable, alive."[4]

When Sofie first came to live with us, we lived on a busy street, and so, I kept the dogs in the house or the back yard. Because the front yard was unfenced, traffic made it unsafe for them. One summer morning, as I potted plants on the front stoop, the dogs were inside, with the screen door closed to keep them secure. Because of Sadie's Old English sheepdog stature, she was able to look out of the top half of the door and scrutinize my activities. But, Sofie, who stood a diminutive eight inches, could only hear the sounds of digging and scraping, watch Sadie, and covet her vantage point. After about ten minutes, I heard an unusual racket— something banging against the door. I looked inside and discovered that little Sofie had dragged an upside down bucket over to the door and climbed up on it to see outside. Sofie the tool user! This was one of many occasions where her active participation was the order of the moment, and she was rightly rewarded for her initiative.

Dogs may choose to *act* or quietly observe. Whichever course they choose, they possess an inherent ability to know which path is the most correct for the moment. It's difficult to discern exactly how they make these choices, but their selections leave them, generally speaking, exercised, rested, stimulated, and at peace with the world. Or, to paraphrase a Krishnamurti dictum, 'They have no need to go anywhere. They are already there.' All in all, they display a well rounded approach to life, one we might do well to emulate.

> *Should one seek at all? Seeking is always for something over there on the other bank, in the distance covered by time . . . The seeking and the finding are in the future—over there, just beyond the hill . . .*

> *All life is in the present, not in the shadow of yesterday or in the brightness of tomorrow's hope. To live in the present one has to be free of the past, and of tomorrow. Nothing is found in the tomorrow, for tomorrow is the present, and yesterday is only a remembrance. So the distance between that which is to be found and that which is, is made ever wider by the search— however pleasant and comforting that search may be . . .*

> *To live in the present the mind must not be divided by the remembrance of yesterday or the bright hope of tomorrow; it must have no tomorrow and no yesterday . . .*

> *The ending [of the old way of thinking] is the beginning, and the beginning is the first step, and the first step is the only step.*[5]
> —*The Second Penguin Krishnamurti Reader*

Continuously feeling the need to *act* can, in many circumstances, produce undesirable results. And, by doing so, in an automatic mode, not only are we prone to influences that could result in a failed endeavor, the outcomes that we do achieve might lack the full essence and significance that we had envisioned. If we strive to contemplate more and act more thoughtfully and lovingly, we allow for higher solutions of greater wisdom to be revealed, as we endeavor to pace ourselves in a serene, enlightened manner.

Rumi, a Sufi mystic in the late thirteenth-century, imparted this discussion with a Sufi wise one. He says, "Secretly we spoke, that wise one and me. I said, 'Tell me the secrets of the world.' The wise one replied, 'Ssssh, let silence tell you the secrets of the world.'"[6]

Helen Keller, who was blind and deaf most of her life, paid a moving tribute to canine sensitivity in *A Tribute to a Dog*.

> *The charming relations I have had with a long succession of dogs results from their happy spontaneity. Usually they are quick to discover that I cannot see or hear. Considerately they rise as I come near, so that I may not stumble. It is not a training but love which impels them to break their silence about me with the thud of a tail rippling against my chair, on gambols round the study, or news conveyed by expressive ear, nose, and paw. Often I yearn to give them speech, their motions are so eloquent with things they cannot say. Truly, as companions, friends, equals in opportunities of self-expression, they unfold to me the dignity of creation, and their joy smiles the blessing of St. Francis.[7]*

When apropos, our canine allies also have a wonderfully natural tenor of actively transforming life. They have an answer to a higher order, as opposed to merely contemplating it. This duality in their nature equips them to handle a broad range of situations—from guiding a blind person through the course of their day, to achieving a dramatic rescue. Dogs are equally capable of responding, instantly, to a circumstance of compelling urgency, or settling in stillness—offering comfort to a companion who is ill or frail, or patiently providing protection for a young child. In other words, they are responsible; they are endowed with the ability to respond.

> *One might say that now exists all the time, beyond the concept of relativity. But since all concepts are based on the idea of relativity, it is impossible to find any words which go beyond that. So nowness is the only way to see directly. First it is between the past and the future — now. Then gradually one discovers that nowness is not dependent on relativity at all . . . The past does not exist, the future does not exist— everything happens now.*[8]
>
> *—Meditation in Action*

Perhaps, when dogs interact with us, in an energetic, active mode, they do so because they do not have the verbal skills to communicate their thoughts and feelings. Regardless, all dogs, whatever their activity level, express a magnitude of emotions, but not with words. They speak with their eyes, their bodies, and their own unique language of sound. And their means of communication are very compelling.

Dundee has an amazing repertoire of sounds that convey a vast range of emotions and desires. An energetic, dramatic communicator; his range is indeed impressive. One evening, I watched a television show about wolves. I thought the dogs might enjoy hearing about their cousins, but they seemed content to snooze. Later that night, when most of the neighborhood was asleep, a group of raucous party-goers could barely be heard in the distance, enjoying their festivities. Little Dundee sprang to life and began howling like a wolf—each howl ended with a delightful squeak, as though he couldn't resist completing each bay with a final flourish. Perhaps a future awaits him making Hollywood doggie soundtracks! Regardless, this dog patter is entertaining and engaging. For many dog aficionados, this uncommon talk endears them to us even more.

It is hard to surpass the capacity of dogs in the realm of authenticity. If you yearn to experience an honest exchange of genuine emotions and actions, spend an afternoon exploring nature with a dog. Their ability and resolve to face all aspects of life with a true, straightforward passion, energizes them and delights their human companions as they actively engage with the creatures and circumstances of their environment. The purity and honesty of their actions suggests a purpose bordering on, if not embracing, the altruistic spirit. The one exception might be when their efforts are concentrated on excavating the flower beds! But, even then, perhaps they are on a sublime mission that is lost on the rest of us.

Dogs care deeply for their family members as well as members of other species. They demonstrate compassion in situations of distress, and generally, seek harmony for the good of all. When we witness that such attributes are possible, they are easier for us to emulate ourselves—to incorporate these values into our own consciousness. Because dogs live so wholly and freely, always wanting to experience more of life, they can inspire us to overcome our fears, our beliefs in limitations, to develop the courage to move forward into a larger, more abundant life.

As we pay less attention to the pulls and pressures of the outer world, we gain the peace and space necessary for the growth of our inner selves. And, as this development unfolds, we can, again, follow the examples of our canine teachers and do something to integrate this increased awareness to improve our lives.

Dogs are distinguished in their capacity for blending 'being' *and* 'doing'. To 'be' and to 'do' concurrently requires a magnificent balance worthy of respect and emulation. Dogs are secure enough within themselves and their place in the world (either 'being' or 'doing') to respond appropriately to their circumstances. Like mystics, dogs never seem to wrestle with a response, but instinctively accomplish what needs to be done from a deep and compassionate knowingness. Their authenticity overrides any insecurity they may feel, and the truth shines through in their actions. They blend their energy with all that is around them and navigate their course based on their inner wisdom and attunement. The direction in which they move is towards unification, contributing to and supporting a greater ethical order.

The time dogs spend in their reflective, receptive state, attuning with smells, sounds, and honing their exceptional intuition, greatly enhances their overall perspective. This clarifies and strengthens both their sense of individuality and their connection to all other beings. Silence helps teach us patience. As Hindu teacher Swami Paramananda taught, "The deep things do not come suddenly. Let us be patient—with ourselves. We may recognize many defects in our natures . . . it can all be removed. Go on working silently."[9]

It is important to remain truthful to our inner directives as we respond honestly and ethically to our everyday experiences. Growth and change can take time to manifest. Small adjustments may be necessary, at first, as we endeavor to remain open to receive more information. These shifts can be greatly obscured, if not totally blocked, when we bombard our sensitivities with the distractions of excessive television, loud music and superficial social interactions. Dogs find contentment with their lives just as they are. They appear to want for nothing, finding joy in simple pleasures, engaging in their surroundings with zest and delight.

Rick Bass, as he searched for and remembered his lost beloved, found the unadulterated passion of his much celebrated superdog, Colter, to be a source of mystery and veneration:

One way or the other, he is still out there running. He will never rest. there will always be this small gulf between us. I will always want him to know a moment's rest, and peace, and he will always know in his hot heart that the only peace to be gotten is by never resting, by always pushing on.[10]

This ability to match the cadence of life seems so effortless for dogs while we humans struggle, analyze, and torment ourselves over the ramifications of even minor events in our lives. Most of our days are spent engaged in a superficial and routine world, the depth and profundity of enlightenment a world away. Animals, in general, seem more advanced in this area of development. They know the value of *right action*, and, in this realm, they can be our guides and mentors.

To achieve this state of peace we may decide to simplify our lives and focus more on the amazing wonders of the world around us.

> *Right action is disinterested action without desire for self-aggrandizement, fame, profit or power. The perfect action is one performed with attention to the action along. . . Right action is seen to lie not in the choice of behaving in this or that way, but in preserving a mindful attitude in all eventualities. The accent throughout is on the moment. What may follow should not be dwelt upon. Desire for results is a sure and destructive enemy of mindfulness.*[11]

Eckhart taught that God is not found in the soul by adding anything, but by a process of subtraction.

Human societies of more aboriginal orientation seem more endowed in this arena as well. Perhaps, because they have not abandoned their links to the miracles of nature around them, they remain more at ease with the cycles of life and at peace with their place in the world. They possess a vitality, abundant and replete with wondrous lifeblood. They can sense that they have all they need (or they wouldn't be here), and they appreciate the precious merit of every moment. As Jeffrey Masson describes his dogs:

> *They turn to watch which way I will go at a fork in the road. They are so interested. It is extraordinary how much interest they can invest in the most ordinary thing. I find it entirely humbling. That concentrated, full, complete, undisturbed interest is what everybody wants from their own human companion.*[12]

Because we have substantially abandoned this true and natural way of energizing our Life Force, the journey towards enlightenment may seem foreign, even dark and uncertain. We are unfamiliar with, and have lost confidence in, many of our natural abilities. Our senses, our intuition, a belief in goodness, a feeling of gratitude, the mettle to take risks, and our ability to feel joy and share love are, too often, foreign concepts in our lives.

According to Coco, the diving dog:

I live for this moment. After the approach and flight, quite honestly, the water is a bit of a let down. Think back to your first kiss. At some point you knew it was going to happen, and soon you'd never be the same. The electricity and confusion of the moment takes over. Every second is as happily painful as it is eternal. I get that feeling every time. The leash comes off and in a flash I know no one can stop me.

I pause, and then fly to the edge without thought of past or future. I would trade every bone I've ever had to live forever in the instant before descent.[13]

—Coco (a.k.a. Dylan Schaffer)

Dogs are patient and fully present for each moment, which gives them the security to welcome the next moment. From them, we can learn to sense what is right and good for us, embrace it and become that goodness.

It is only out of the mystical tradition that our prophetic work to transform society will be authentically radical, will be rooted. Authentic action comes out of non-action. It comes out of respect for mystery and wonder and the gift and the glorious surprise of our being here.[14]

—Matthew Fox

I think we are drawn to dogs because they are the uninhibited creatures we might be if we weren't certain we knew better.[15]

—George Bird Evans, author (b.1906)

Chapter 7

COMPASSION AND GIVING

*The purpose of this world is not "to have and to hold," but
"to give and to serve." There can be no other meaning.*
                                        —Sir Wilfred T. Grenfell

I hope to be the kind of person my dog thinks I am.
                                        —Author unknown

Because of their innate capacity to bestow love, enthusiasm, goodness and devotion, some dog enthusiasts deem dogs to be angels manifested in animal form. There are endless accounts of their unceasing capacity to give, often at their own peril. They transcend the world of selfish, individual motivation to inhabit a realm of loving generosity.

Wolves have been known to suckle lost children; dogs have saved humans from perilous situations, often sacrificing their own lives. Guide dogs provide sight, touch, and hearing to the disabled and grant them an expanded world of freedom. Therapy dogs offer solace, safety, and serenity to the emotionally fragile. There are accounts of dogs leading people to safety, then disappearing without a trace. Is it any wonder they are considered by many to be angels on earth?

Perhaps mankind, through the domestication of dogs, has established perpetual numbers of kind teachers and guides to help us learn and live this most valuable lesson. For those who can be humble and open, dogs provide us a safe space to look at ourselves honestly. Through their accepting and supporting ways, they give us the freedom to make the choices and mistakes from which meaningful changes can occur.

Dogs seem to possess these traits inherently, but, for humans, struggling to find a spiritual footing, the process can be a challenging journey. Sophy Burnham describes the essence of a "real" spiritual encounter:

- *A feeling of being in a wider life than world's selfish interest,*

- *A sense of the goodness and friendliness of the universe, and a surrender to that will,*

- *An immense elation and fearlessness in acting; a shedding of all vain, selfish, or egotistical goals.*

- *A tenderness toward all things; a shifting of the center toward loving and harmonious relationships, toward "yes, yes," and away from anxious, prideful "no."*[1]

Dogs, at times, seem to absorb and internalize our upheavals as their own. Their empathic natures sense our feelings, and they respond in kind. Experiencing this symbiotic identification with our concerns touches our hearts and provides us solace. Knowing that our grief or loneliness is shared eases our burden and can give us a renewed sense of hope and serenity.

Our canine cohabitants demonstrate the interconnectedness of all things, and share that wonderful discovery as if their entire beings were a part of everything in their environment. Even if they receive nothing in return, love prevails. Indeed, under these circumstances, dogs have been known to make great sacrifices to others in need. They connect from the heart, not from a power base, and thus, their souls grow and evolve and mentor us to do the same. Because they come from a state of harmony and balance, dogs create a world of peace and acceptance around them.

During my tenure as a social worker on the Flathead Reservation in western Montana during the 1980's, I assisted the elderly who were at risk of abuse or neglect. One of my clients, I'll call her Nellie, lived by herself in a rustic cabin on the outskirts of Ronan. She had lived her entire life alone, but, when I knew her, she had the abiding company of her dog, Cub, and a countless variety of cats, some feral, others contentedly tranquil and well established fixtures in her household. By modern standards she lived a primitive life. She heated her house with wood, and cooked for the entire animal crew on an old-fashioned woodstove. Due to her cantankerous nature, Nellie had few visitors and no one to assist her with the chores of daily living. Rough encounters with her more brazen cats left her with open, unhealing sores on her legs and arms. She scoffed at the suggestion of medical care and nursed her wounds with her own home remedies. Wisps of cat hair clung to every object in the house, including the teacups that she invariably offered, half filled with her famous, unidentifiable brew.

Crusty and tough, Nellie refused to relinquish this colorful life for the safe, sterile security of a supervised living apartment. Since I heated my own house with wood, I was well accustomed to the ritual of gathering and splitting wood. I would visit her on the weekends, replenish her wood supply, and share the capers of her own private animal kingdom. Nellie's spats with her cats were always the chief topic of conversation, often complete with a demonstration. And, throughout, Cub provided them all with his calm, accepting presence. The kinship that those animals provided Nellie indisputably gave her life meaning and substance, motivation to face each day. The cats fueled her soul and satisfied her need for pugnacious relations. And, throughout the upheavals, Cub sat patiently at her feet, quietly observing. He was a rock-solid force in her life.

Nellie's life illustrated that we create what we are, from what we believe, and these revelations come in the present, not the future. Nellie had a rough-hewn, difficult, but satisfying life, and Cub and her cats stayed the course.

Dogs' greatest desire is to *give*—purely, from their hearts. It is only through the gift of love, the benefaction of their personalities, that their calling can be completed. Their passions satisfied. Many years later, ensconced in the comfort of the woods near Bozeman, I was fortunate to share my days with my own canine guardian and mentor, a large soul in a small dog body named Sofie who, like Cub did with Nellie, marked my daily activities. She gave Sadie and me what we needed to feel appreciated and at ease. Whenever I left the house for the evening, upon my return, Sofie was there with an enthusiastic greeting, sprinting up the stairs, her entire body wiggling—a smile in her eyes. Then, she would scamper around until she found one of her toys and bring it to me, delighted to present her 'welcome home' offering. And, to complete the cycle, the love she offered generated an instantaneous and equally loving response.

To reciprocate this devotion, it seems fitting that we return these kindnesses and do our part to create a world of safety and love for the good of all sentient beings. We can accomplish this by celebrating the joys of others, finding peace with former enemies, being fully engaged with and comforting those who struggle or grieve.

But what if this spark of friendliness refuses to kindle? A follower of Ouspensky's complained that he could not feel love for anyone and asked where to begin. "Begin with the dog," was the advice he received.[2] Dogs have been the steady and loyal companions to humans for almost 20,000 years. If we continue on this track, we will enjoy plenitude of opportunities to return these kind gestures. As Evans-Wentz counsels, "As long as the sky endureth, so long will there be no end of sentient beings for one to serve; and to everyone cometh the opportunity for such service."[3]

The desire of dogs to satisfy their own needs becomes secondary to demonstrating the meaningful service of their love and loyalty towards those in need. When Sofie was still very young—about five months—she accompanied me to a lavish wedding and reception. My friends, Nancy and Sharon, and I camped on a lake shore in the Swan Valley with Sofie and Sadie, my Old English Sheepdog. Captivated by the changing light of eventide, I tossed a stick into the chilly, October waters and coaxed Sadie to fetch it. She contemplated the branch, distant in the waves and decided on a more sedentary activity—watching. She was, apparently, engaged in a contemplative moment.

All the while, Sofie carefully observed this scene. Finally, when she was certain that Sadie was not going to collect the stick, Sofie swam out and reclaimed it. The endeavor seemed to take forever, as her tiny legs made slow progress against the forces of the immense lake. But, her determination eventually paid off. She retrieved the stick, and, bobbing and deliberately creeping through the gray waves, delivered it back to shore. Dripping wet and chilled, she laid it at Sadie's feet, respectful of Sadie's dominant status. We all watched in amazement—not only at such a brave feat for a young puppy, but the deference that she showed towards the older dog.

Dogs have their own unique knowledge and vision—a mission of compassion, love and empathy. And, they carry forth this teeming capacity for Life into their entire world. The Dalai Lama believes, "In one sense one could define compassion as the feeling of unbearableness at the sight of other people's suffering, other sentient being's suffering. And in order to generate that feeling one must first have an appreciation of the seriousness or intensity of another's suffering. So, I think that the more fully one understands, and the various kinds of suffering that we are subject to, the deeper will be one's level of compassion."[4]

In my experience, all but the most jaded individuals are inspired to respect and reciprocate these canine beatitudes, often with gratitude for the experience. In his book *Understanding Your Dog*, Eberhard

Trumler concludes that the true nature of the dog is an innate requirement for friendly contact with others. In the canine temperament, it could almost be called an instinct, it is so hard to extinguish.[5]

And, Milan Kundera reminds us, in his book, *The Unbearable Lightness of Being*, that we humans certainly need work in this area:

> *True human goodness, in all its purity and freedom, can come to the fore only when its recipient has no power. Mankind's true moral test, its fundamental test (which lies deeply buried from view), consists of its attitude towards those who are at its mercy: animals. And in this respect has suffered a fundamental debacle, a debacle so fundamental that all others stem from it.*[6]

Dogs give of themselves in a most genuine and generous way, asking nothing in return, confident that the Universe provides for their needs. And, in turn, they hold the wisdom to receive—to complete this important cycle. Their strongest emotional desire is to give, even if it means denying their own needs. Dogs' innate connection between emotions and sensory expression confers a broad range of emotional display. James Thurber witnessed this many years ago.

> *The effect upon the dog of his life with Man is discernible in his eyes, which frequently are capable of a greater range of expression than Man's. The eyes of the sensitive French poodle, for example, can shine with such an unalloyed glee and darken with so profound a gravity as to disconcert the masters of the earth, who have lost the key to so many of the simpler magics. Man has practiced for such a long time to mask his feelings and to regiment his emotions that some basic quality of naturalness has gone out of both his gaiety and his solemnity. The dog is aware of this, I think. You can see it in his eyes sometimes when he lies and looks at you with a long rueful gaze.*[7]

And, because of dogs' dependence on us, both real and perceived, the greater our responsibility becomes to provide for their care, to honor their spirit, and to not betray the trust they so openly extend to us. In response to their carefree innocence, we learn to be more caring and empathetic. As the Dalai Lama says, "So, no matter how much violence or how many bad things we have to go through, I believe that the ultimate solution to our conflicts, both internal and external, lies in returning to our basic or underlying human nature, which is gentle and compassionate."[8]

Many people treat their dogs like they would their children, but they may be hesitant to reveal the tremendous role that dogs plays in their lives. This is a remarkable relationship, one that could be a source of pride and inspiration to others. Often, their dog friends are the only repository available to share love and closeness. But, this extraordinary bond can be tremendously beneficial to both allies. If your dog is a special and treasured friend, sharing this with others might inspire them to seek a similar alliance of their own.

Part of the special closeness we share with dogs is the exchange of physical touch. When Sadie was a young dog, she exhibited many of the behaviors that are characteristic in children with attachment disorders. She came to live with me at the age of five months and, due to a variety of circumstances, I offered her the fifth home in her short life. Although her prior human care-givers had met all of her physical needs, it was clear that Sadie had not received the attention necessary to develop a secure emotional base. She did not appear bonded to anyone, and, given any chance, she would run off, completely out of my sight, until some concerned passerby would contain her, allowing me to catch up. For months, I took her for walks in a vast expanse of trails on the edge of town, where she would be safe if she did vanish over the horizon. Over time, and with much love and patience, Sadie and I were able to break through these trust barriers. Hours of petting, stroking, and calm reassurance finally helped Sadie realize that she was loved and wanted, that she had a home where she belonged. And, I learned how critical physical touch can be in soothing the soul and forming the bonds of mutual regard.

It is clear that dogs like to be touched, in some ways more than others. For male dogs especially, having their chests scratched between their front legs transports them to their own version of nirvana. It is believed that this action replicates the sensations the male dog experiences during breeding, with his chest in contact with the back of the female. Most every dog enjoys being scratched behind the ears. Cuddling is equally welcomed, perhaps reminding the dog of the days and nights it nestled with its litter mates. In any event, physical contact is usually well received and serves to strengthen the bonds of trust and affection. A well known saying sums this up: "What is not given is lost," so scratch, cuddle and snuggle! Your dog friends will be ever so grateful.

From our interactions with dogs, we can assimilate a gentler, more compassionate manner in our dealings with others, including our animal friends. We can resolve to befriend stray or mistreated animals, volunteer at a local humane society, and give a lonely or frightened dog the gift of our time and concern. As the Zen monk, Thich Nhat Hanh, shares: "We may need to transform suffering into insight, insight into nonduality, insight that leads to compassion."[9] These acts of kindness return to us, often in mysterious ways, but the fulfillment of touch is instantaneous.

George Picher and Ed Cone describe their relationship with a stray dog, Lupa, in their book *The Dogs Who Came to Stay*. For months she warily guarded her seven pups in a remote part of their yard and would not allow any close contact. But, their loving persistence eventually won her over, and, as she gained trust, she eventually became a central figure in their lives along with her pup, Remus:

> *On the one hand, we loved her and cared for her as parents love and care for their child. But on the other hand, she was also, for us, a mother figure. I'm not quite sure what that*

means, but I'm certain it's true. Part of what it means, I think, is this: we felt that as long as she was there, we were in some inexplicable way, if not exactly safe from harm, then at least watched over and generally speaking okay.

Lupa gave them her greatest gifts, benefactions beyond monetary measure: her love and compassion, and mostly, her *presence* in their lives. But, the love and trust that they shared with Lupa began with their extension of care and concern towards her.[10]

Hosea promotes the concept of Isaiah's vision of the peaceable kingdom. In this prophecy he foresees a future when animals will not be killed by humans:

In that day I will make a covenant for them; With the beast of the field and the birds of the air and the creatures that move along the ground. Bow and sword and battle I will abolish from the land So that all may lie down in safety.
—(Hosea 2:18)

The image of a peaceable kingdom, like a beacon lighting our path, helps us find the roots of our spiritual origins. We discover an awareness that all life is sacred and interrelated, and that all living beings deserve our compassion. And, in return, through our newfound awareness, we might find the peaceable kingdom within ourselves.[11]

Compassion is rarely found in the lives of the complacent. Matthew Fox relates how compassion is a kind of *fire* that disturbs, surprises, ignites, burns, sears and warms. "Compassion incinerates denial; it especially warms and melts cold hearts, cold structures, frozen minds, and self-satisfied life-styles. Those who are touched by compassion have their lives turned upside down. That is not necessarily a bad thing."[12]

I love a dog. He does nothing for political reasons.
—Will Rogers

65

Chapter 8

FORGIVENESS

To err is human: To forgive, canine.

—Author unknown

*My dogs forgive anger in me, the arrogance in me, the brute
in me. They forgive everything I do before I forgive myself.*

—Guy de la Valdene, author

In 1903, Maurice Maeterlinck published a compact classic entitled *Our Friend the Dog*. He observed, "The dog succeeds in piercing, in order to draw closer to us, the partitions, ever elsewhere impermeable, that separate the species! We are alone, absolutely alone on this planet; and amid all the forms of life that surround us, not one, excepting the dog, has made an alliance with us. . . The dog is really a privileged animal. He is the only living being that has found and recognizes an indubitable, tangible, unexceptionable and definite god."[1] But, we humans, in the role of "God", with all the potency and obligation we may feel towards our dogs, so often let them down.[2]

As Allen Shoen reflected, "That evening at sunset I looked out over the calm waters and wondered how many species of animals would relate to us in special ways if they had not had prior harmful experiences. What would our lives be like if all animals had an oppor-

67

tunity to share their love with us, if they could approach us without fear of death?"[3]

Does our own self-hate project itself onto our external world? Do we disdain and assail in others, our very own shortcomings—those we attempt to conceal even from ourselves. The evolution of all creatures suffers as a result.

Renowned author and veterinarian James Herriot once treated a young dog that had been chained to a wall, inside a dark, desolate shed for almost a year:

> *I had seen some thin dogs but this advanced emaciation reminded me of my text books on anatomy; nowhere else did the bones of pelvis, face and rib cage stand out with such horrifying clarity. A deep, smoothed-out hollow in the earth floor showed where he had lain, moved about, in fact lived for a very long time. . . I carefully raised the dog from his sitting position and realized that the stench in the place was not entirely due to the piles of excrement. The hindquarters were a welter of pressure sores which had turned gangrenous, and strips of sloughing tissue hung down from them. There were similar sores along the sternum and ribs.*[4]

Herriot, accompanied by an inspector, learned that the dog had been in the shed since he was an eight week old pup. He was sickened at the thought of this patient animal sitting starved and forgotten in the darkness and filth for a year. But, when he looked at the dog, he "saw in his eyes only a calm trust . . . the kind that had complete faith in people and accepted all their actions without complaint."[5] The inspector assumed that Herriot would euthanize the dog right away. Herriot thought for a moment and agreed. He knew he could never find a home for the dog in that condition.

When the door to the shed was opened fully, they discovered the dog was a Golden Retriever. At the same time, a local resident, Mrs.

Donovan, known for her amazing home remedies, happened by and assisted with the rescue. She was immediately drawn to the dog and begged to keep him and make him better. Initially doubtful, but after some close scrutiny and deliberation, the inspector finally consented. Weeks passed before Mrs. Donovan was seen again, but when she appeared, she had with her, a big yellow dog, looking bright and happy. His wounds were healing and his skin and coat were clean. This eccentric, dumpy little figure was brimming with pride because she made a difference to this dog![6]

As this story depicts, dogs are able to forgive, even when they have been severely mistreated. When Sadie, the huge sheepdog, accidentally caused Sofie or Scotia pain, they showed no desire to retaliate, to perpetrate guilt or prolonged ill-will. Placing *blame* did not seem to be a part of their countenance. In fact, after recovering from their initial response to feeling pain, they would often make a conciliatory gesture, almost immediately, offering forgiveness, eager to keep the peace and reestablish harmony.

Dogs continue to trust and love, wanting to maintain peace with their companions, and, through their kindly actions, they inspire us to do the same. Conversely, when dogs have committed a deed that incurs our displeasure, they seem acutely relieved when they are forgiven and welcomed back into our good graces.

Forgiveness is necessary to achieve inner peace, and, again, dogs can be our ever present teachers. As we strive to practice non-attachment to specific results, to release the pain of our past, we arrive at a balanced state which calms our emotions and comforts our souls. Sadie will often watch her surroundings for long periods of time, absorbing the essence of the situation. Whenever we walk down by the creek in the backyard, she goes directly to the spot where we found Sofie's body and gazes into the water, lost in her thoughts. As she turns away, I wonder what she is thinking. Is she, too, attempting to make sense of the unfathomable?

Some dogs manage to overcome extreme trauma with a strong resilience, a shield that allows them to continue on their mission of love, tolerance and acceptance. They are able to tap an inner fortitude which somehow sustains them through the abuse, strengthening them to survive these ordeals. They learn self reliance and, unless they are extremely mistreated, do not withdraw into a solitary, fearful existence. They seemingly use these trials to enhance their fortitude and expand the knowledge of what their inner depths can accomplish.

Philosopher, Tom Regan, tells the story of his college roommate who was assigned a dog in his surgery class on whom he would perform a variety of procedures. "He described to me how he broke the poor animal's leg and then set it, only to break it again. Throughout her long, painful ordeal, the loyal animal greeted his arrival with a wag of her tail and even licked the very hands that had injured her. In the end, after he had studied one or another thing about her treatment and recovery, he was required to 'euthanize' the dog. It did not sit well with him. He thought it cruel and unnecessary. He wanted to speak out, to object, but he lacked the courage. He wondered what sort of human being he was or would become."[7] This mind-set, promulgated in many medical schools, research labs and western thought in general, has its roots in the teachings of Descartes, who promoted the notion that humans have the right to "use" animals because they (humans) occupy the top position of the hierarchy.[8]

We don't know if the medical student gathered the courage to save the dog from death, but it seemed clear that the dog's affection and acceptance of him had ultimately increased his awareness of her suffering. And, we do know that spiritual development is built on the foundation of awareness and compassion. Awareness triggers compassionate action, and compassion perfects and deepens awareness.

Dogs think, intuit and act, and following their own inner guidance, tap into the Universal sense of order and harmony. Matthew Fox is so taken with the divine place that animals have in this world, he proposes celebrations, rituals and liturgies to pay homage to their contributions. John Seed and Joanna Macy have created the Council of All Beings that takes you into the grief about the extinction of species. Some churches have an annual commemoration where the congregations can bring their animal friends to be blessed.

But, Fox's veneration would praise animals and seek their blessing, "Yet I've always been repelled by the notion that animals need our blessing. Animals don't need our blessing, we need their blessing. It should be blessing from the animals—that would be the real praise, instead of blessing *of* the animals."[9]

Jeffrey Masson recalls his encounters with racing greyhounds and their remarkable capacity to overcome the abuse they have suffered, and maintain a loving, accepting posture towards humans. Although they are gentle, they are never socialized. They are kept in cages their entire careers. They suffer from beatings and lack of attention, yet they are able to forgive and to seek friendship. He was deeply moved at their gentle demeanor, their gaze of absolute trust and sweetness. "Racing greyhounds are neglected and abused, then simply discarded, like so much rubbish, yet the emotion they so clearly manifest is forgiveness."[10]

Masson likens it to the story that appeared in 1842, in a book entitled, *Animal Biography*. The story originally appeared in a French newspaper:

A young man took a dog into a boat, rowed to the center of the Seine, and threw the animal over, with intent to drown him. The poor dog often tried to climb up the side of the boat; his master as often pushed him back, till overbalancing himself, he fell overboard. As soon as the faithful dog saw his master in the stream, he left the boat and held him above water till help arrived from the shore, and his life was saved. This, and countless other tales of the loving capacity of dogs, affirm Masson's belief that, "It just seems in their nature to go on loving through all their experiences, even the worst."[11] Dogs send us the message of forgiveness loud and clear. Our lesson is to hear it, and then, as we proceed through life, to make it a part of our own conduct.

> *Man's capacity for suffering tends to increase in depth and subtlety with the increase of culture and civilization; ignores the still more mysterious, perhaps most significant circumstance that the highest types have accepted it eagerly and willingly, have found in Pain, the grave but kindly teacher of immortal secrets, the conferrer of liberty, ever the initiator into amazing joys.*[12]
>
> —Evelyn Underhill

> *The Via Creativa is always about making mistakes and even celebrating and learning to recycle them. From mistakes arise diversity and new possibilities. We often learn what is most important by trial and error . . . We can strive for excellence without being addicted to perfection; the two are not the same thing. Excellence is about being the best and the most beautiful that we can be; perfection presumes an outside norm for what is best, ignoring the subjective, the personal, and the unique.*[13]
>
> —Matthew Fox

Chapter 9

TOLERANCE AND PATIENCE

*To endure all things with an equable and peaceful mind not
only brings many blessings to the soul; but it also enables us,
amid difficulties, to have a clear judgement and remedy them
in the most fitting way.*

—John of the Cross, The Dark Night

The bounty of any friendship broadens our soul, and we can
accelerate this process through interactions with our canine companions. When we are fortunate enough to make this connection of good-
will, of common and abiding concern, our lives and our view of love
are changed forever. Because dogs accept us as we are, with all our
faults and frailties, we are free to express our true selves, to drop our
guard, and open our hearts to receive their love and affection. Perhaps,
for the first time in our lives, we experience total acceptance and
unconditional positive regard, flexibility, constancy and patience. And
for those willing to receive it, it can be one of the greatest blessings of
a lifetime.

Dogs demonstrate that a key remedy to help relieve our fears
and inhibitions is to openly express our emotions—to live each
moment to the fullest, to accept our circumstances for what they are,
and make the most of them. Dogs have conquered this realm, and so,

possess the mastery to be our guides. By their spontaneous actions, they teach us how to enjoy the simplest pleasures of life: a walk in the woods, the scents of each season, the warmth of the sun as it enfolds the earth. We relive the innocence of our childhood, how each day was an adventure in growth and learning. Dogs connect us with those memories, and remind us to live without judging; to accept each of life's lessons as perfect for what we need at that moment.

Because dogs' raison d'etre is to express love and bestow joy and devotion, this exudes strongly from their souls and in their personalities. Their innate joyful state emerges because of this presence of love. Dogs hold within themselves a state of inner peace, a tolerance towards all that surrounds them. They are able to give and receive freely, with acceptance and gratitude. They listen to the guidance of their hearts and reach out with an abundance of friendliness, patience, and forgiveness.

Any power struggles in which dogs may engage are usually invoked to provide for their basic survival requirements: sustenance, defending their young, or responding to a threat or challenge. Yet, they limit the encounter to only what is necessary to put the situation right. They have no need or desire to perpetuate unnecessary conflict.

Dogs express what is true, with sincerity, from their hearts. And if we model this behavior, they can help us open our hearts as well. Intuition, and responding with inherent emotions, shapes and guides their authentic healing ways. In a most natural and genuine manner, they help us eliminate the obstacles we perceive (or create), that prevent our full experience of love and life. Our canine consorts wait patiently as we struggle with our demons; they help us heal our emotional wounds, accepting us, regardless of our flaws.

Their affirmations assist us in believing that we can become whole. The energy from their generous hearts and their strong will to live inspires us. Dogs help us build courage, and strengthen our own motivation to seek goodness. This powerful, loving exchange can sustain us through the most difficult situations. Because of their strong loyalty, dogs will remain true to us, in situations when our human companions may abandon us.

Just as they are advanced practitioners of forgiveness, dogs also have an amazing capacity for tolerance. They accept circumstances of our lives that our human friends and family might reject, and they will endure conditions that might cause others to fret or complain. It seems inherent within dog nature to manage with what *is*—give a wag of their tail, and make the best of it.

John Steinbeck, in his classic *Travels with Charley*, chronicled his adventures with his dog, as they completed a journey that spanned the continental United States. He recalls Charley's response, when they were caught in the fury of hurricane Donna:

> *Charley dog had no nerves. Gunfire or thunder, explosions or high winds leave him utterly unconcerned. In the midst of the howling storm, he found a warm place under a table and went to sleep.*[1]

Perhaps dogs have a greater insight (or even a sense of humor) into our hapless conduct, than we give them credit for. As Steinbeck described it, "I've seen a look in dogs' eyes, a quickly vanishing look of amazed contempt, and I am convinced that basically dogs think humans are nuts."[2]

Regardless of how dogs might interpret our behaviors, they don't display the desire to condemn us, but rather, they support us with their tolerance, as we encounter the lessons of our lives. We may continue to make the same mistakes, over and over, until we surmount these hurdles, and, by observing our foibles, dogs might even offer a prompt, to cue us in a different direction. But throughout the arduous process, we can be assured that our canine companions will not abandon us as we muddle along, charting our course.

By striving to increase our capacity for tolerance and the acceptance of our own surroundings (including the people we contact daily, either in close relationships or casual contacts), and remaining open to diversity and change, our lives become more relaxed, eminently more splendid and absorbing.

Be willing to take risks, as dogs do so well, to open up your world. Westie puppy, Scotia, has interminable persistence when faced with the many lessons that young lives encounter. She delights in exploring new possibilities (including climbing trees) in her daily routine. And even when she doesn't achieve the results she seeks, she behaves as if she truly gained from the experience—perhaps even enjoyed it, regardless. If we adapt similar habits, the sweeping magnitude of patience will help increase our receptivity to new ideas and solutions: to the challenges we face, to the sources of love in our lives, and the grand adventures that daily living presents.

Scotia's persistence in finding ways to escape from the yard has resulted in more hours of fencing and hole-patching than might be spent to contain a bison bull! Her need to explore and discover, follows the path of her departed sister-spirit, Sofie. One afternoon last October, Scotia was barking frantically and jumping at the bottom of a large fir tree. She had treed a mother black bear and her two cubs. The mother bear was hissing, obviously growing impatient at this intrusion of their apple scavenging. Fortunately, Scotia was retrieved before she became the bears' main course for lunch!

Dogs are our marvelous, gentle mirrors. They show us what we need to see the most. Our superficial preoccupations fall away, and what is real and important shines through. Dogs appear to have very few expectations; they let us be who and what we really are. They don't wait for us to love them. They encourage us to join them in their charming, altruistic dance, but, at the same time, they respect our fragile boundaries. We are welcomed to discover and explore, in the realm of their gentle acceptance, the areas in which our hearts are closed. And we can do this at our own pace, knowing they won't reject us.

By facing and overcoming these emotional barriers, we glimpse the path of unconditional love. The tolerance that dogs possess allows them to remain calm and accepting, regardless of the chaos around them. They allow us to make mistakes and still receive the safe space of their love. When we accept this challenge and follow their fine example, we discover that there is no need to conceal our flaws. We can present our unique gifts without having to defend them or apologize. Thus, our path through life is quieted. It requires less effort for others to relax and be themselves around us. This safe harbor serves everyone's healing; we begin to view the world as secure and full of possibilities. The link to our intuition becomes clearer and more reliable. We feel enhanced, perhaps even a yearning to play, or take a risk or two. We discover that, just as dogs exude this superb attribute, so can we find ourselves; so can we be love.

As our canine companions continue to share our lives, with all the highs and lows, we are blessed with their capacity for patience. We learn how important this quality is in the evolution of our souls. In the words of the Dalai Lama, "When you are engaged in the practice of patience and tolerance, in reality, what is happening is you are engaged in a combat with hatred and anger."[3]

From my own personal experience, I believe this to be an eminent and core truth. It is one of the most profound lessons I have faced, and one of the most challenging. Countless times, I have rushed, unprepared, into a situation, desiring a certain outcome and feeling determined, by God, to make it happen. Rather than paying attention to subtle information that might be present and pertinent, I convince myself that events should proceed along a certain course and then set about to make that happen. Occasionally, the whole undertaking works out for 'the best.' But, more often than not, when using this approach, I am left feeling unsettled—wondering, if I had allowed more time for the experience to unfold in a more natural and complete manner, perhaps the results might have been considerably more satisfying.

Dogs are, also, masters of patience. Dogs wait. They wait for us all of the time. As Gary Stanley describes this, "Ever watch a dog in wait mode? It's pretty much what dogs do. They wait for you to get up. They wait to be let out. They wait to go for a walk. They wait to be fed. They wait for you to come home. They wait."[4]

But, often, it is the dog of the household who has the greatest knowledge of what truly goes on. The real state of affairs. Through their silent observations, they absorb and recall our habits to the minutest detail. Time and again, it seems they might know us even better than we know ourselves. But, as Stanley sees it, "Waiting is an active exercise of hope, born of careful observation over time that produces a deep understanding of who or what is being waited for. Waiting is a skill well worth developing. Few things offer such attractive rewards as waiting . . . Waiting isn't being put on hold. Waiting is a matter of taking hold."[5]

During the many years I spent with Cuya, I absorbed a wealth of wisdom from observing her in action. She possessed an archetypal, maternal spirit, raising her litter of handsome puppies with abiding attention and patience. She endured their demands, even though she was weak from an infection that left her gravely ill. When Cuya was five years old, already a longstanding stalwart of reliability, she and her son, Little Bear, remained on the farm, ensconced on the west shore of Flathead Lake, with only minimal care and supervision, while I spent six weeks in Europe. Cuya, so comfortable and secure in almost any setting, conveyed her peaceful serenity and confident nature to her son. They ran free and unfettered in nature, communing with the horses, chickens and pheasants, flushing out badgers—living the kind of life that Old English Sheepdogs relish.

I couldn't bear to compound any feelings of abandonment Cuya might experience by, not only leaving her, but confining her in a strange place while I was gone. So, I made arrangements with my trustworthy friend, Jan, to board the dogs in the event that they did not adjust. But, Jan reported to me that each day, when she went to the farm to check on the dogs and feed them, there they were, always right by the house, satisfied and serene—waiting. When I returned, after being gone for weeks, I drove up the lane that circled the old farm house. The foot high grass marked the scope of my absence. But, in the midst of the overgrowth, two fluffy white heads turned to meet the sound—my steadfast escort, bobbing and panting, one on each side of the car.

As a young dog, before her pups were born, Cuya was my constant companion. I rarely went anywhere without her. She was a recurrent visitor, even at my workplace, where she received lavish praise and attention. During my time away from work, I spent regular intervals reading and writing, interspersed with my adventures with Cuya. She, invariably, discerned the telltale signs that indicated we were going somewhere—finding my coat, the rattle of keys—she was ready to go, waiting by the door. The table, where I sat to read and write, was in full view of the front door. Over time I noticed, as I sat at the table—lost in some reverie, that even when I *thought* about going somewhere, Cuya would get up, station herself by the door, and study me in ready anticipation. What clue did I give her? None, perhaps, but her patience (and possible telepathy) had endowed her with an erudition of my habits—an awareness of the open door to the joys of her life—our time together. She *knew*; and she let me know that she knew; and so, we departed.

If, somehow, we can enter the world of dog wisdom, our reward is a glimpse of healing energy and love unbounded. It is up to us to recognize and receive these gifts, and, if we so choose, incorporate them into our own sense of self. This can help advance us from our world of fear and uncertainty and open our hearts to a greater, more gratifying world than what we presently inhabit. Some consider dogs to be our "familiars"—abiding attendant spirits that often appear in animal form. Familiars become our teachers, confidantes, and companions; they bring indescribable richness to our lives.

Quite often, ours is a limited view, dominated by a rational interpretation, narrow in vision. Dogs' acts of kindness and loyalty, of playfulness and joy, help heal our hearts and strengthen our ability, in turn, to act with love and tolerance towards others. Each loving act is amplified as it transmits into the world. And, if we follow this path, the energy returns to us, perhaps in a form we may not expect, but that is the grace, the mystery of living. It is a transcendent journey—reborn each moment, fresh and alive, in some pristine, new form.

> *In a wonderland they lie,*
> *Dreaming as the days go by*
> *Dreaming as the summers die.*
>
> *Ever drifting down the stream—*
> *Lingering in the golden gleam—*
> *Life, what is it but a dream?*[6]

—Willie Morris

Chapter 10

When Death Touches Our Own

In dark hours, your silence may be of more help than many two-legged comforters.

—W. H. Auden, poet, to his dog, Rolfi

To forgive ourselves for our transgressions is the work of the soul. Because animals often suffer illness or accident or die in our care, they can serve as excellent missionaries to a place of reconciliation, healed grief, and forgiveness. Often, I believe animals come to our lives specifically to deliver this intimate gift, the awesome gift of their passing.[1]

—Susan Chernak McElroy

As we voyage down life's winding road, we face varied lessons, endowments for the evolution of our souls. Some are pleasant, robust and life-affirming. Many come in the form of challenges and, perhaps, cause us to ponder the meaning of life. These events of our lives are mandatory for our growth: mentally, emotionally and spiritually—to help us leave this world stronger and wiser than we came. None of the lessons we encounter is as agonizing, yet revealing, as the experience of death. It can rock us to the core of our being, but, the definitive apex of the knowledge of life is ultimately fashioned by meeting the process of death.

Each time one of my beloved canine companions departed this world, I felt as though a part of me had died; the grief was so intense, the pull so powerful. However, by cycling through the stages of grief, I discovered that love still held the essence of the relationship ardently, within my heart. Life had merely changed forms.

The day following her death, to honor Sofie and all that she brought to our lives, I sent this message to my friends:

> *I regret to say that last night my beloved, delightful, remarkable little Westie, Sofie, fell through the ice on the creek in our yard and drowned. It was almost dark when I noticed that she was missing. I followed her tracks to an opening in the ice, breaking through the three inch frozen barrier, the freezing water up to my waist. I broke through the ice down to the edge of the property and, for what seemed an eternity, began to backtrack. When I reached the area where I believe she fell in, I found her, floating in the white icy chunks, but by then she was gone.*
>
> *I called the vet and she said there wasn't much that could be done. In desperation, consumed with disbelief, I did CPR on her for almost an hour, and tried to warm with a heating pad, but it was too late. The vet said that animals don't revive from cold water drownings, the way humans sometimes do.*
>
> *It's hard to convey what an extraordinary, devoted influence she has been in our lives. She was the epitome of love, delight and happiness, and she spread it everywhere she went. It's hard to believe that she won't come bounding into the room to check things out. She was so alert; she always seemed to know what was going on around here—more than any of us.*

She loved chasing squirrels and playing with the neighbor dogs. Basically, she loved life so much and brought joy to everyone around her. She was an especially wonderful presence in my life this past year with all of the stress and uncertainty regarding my work.

I will miss her greatly. Hopefully we can keep alive her uncommon qualities that enriched our lives during her time here. This is a huge loss in my life and we are in shock. Sadie seems sad and lost. My bright shining star still glows, but now, she is in another dimension.

It helps me to venerate my esteem for her by putting this down in writing. Remember to appreciate the pure and worthy things in your life, and take them not for granted.

Sofie's life was brief in terms of a Westie's expected life span; she was only three years old when she fell into those dark, icy waters. Throughout our time together, she and I helped each other explore our needs, and discover delightful solutions. But, on that cold winter evening, all of my efforts would not bring her back.

In the days after Sofie was gathered, I visited the creek and recalled our time together. Chunks of icy slush drifted past, bobbing and glimmering, like clumps of diamonds against the charcoal waters. In a numbed state, I finally had to accept the fact that it was Sofie's time to move on, to proceed ahead—to move into the Light. I endeavored to find the strength to give her release. I had to set her free.

A week to the day of Sofie's passing, an astonishing experience occurred, that I also shared with my friends:

Last night marked one week from the day Sofie drowned. I was sitting down by the creek at dusk, about the same time that I discovered her missing—a hat pulled down low over my eyes. As the view darkened, I noticed a bird fly very low across my plane of vision and then land high atop a tree, in a row of tall evergreens across the creek.

Sofie's burial spot is at the end of that row of trees. I rose, curious for a closer look and discovered that the visitor was an owl. There are many forms of wildlife on the property, but, even though I have heard owls many times in the tall cottonwoods, I had never actually seen one. At first I was struck by the similarity of the silhouette to Sofie's shape—a round body with two little pointed ears. The owl sat there, at the tiptop of the tree, looking around, checking things out just like Sofie always did.

Watching this feathered sentinel, I stayed by the water for at least twenty minutes. The owl never moved. Finally, even though I was bundled up, the damp chill settled in my bones. Reluctantly, I started back for the house. Trudging through the crusted drifts, whenever I turned around, I could see the owl perched in the tree. Even from inside the house, with the lights off, I could still discern the form of the owl.

I called a friend who is a nature guide, and very knowledgeable about animal spirituality. She said owls are believed by some to be messengers. That sometimes the departed soul returns in physical form, usually four to nine days after death, before becoming immersed as a part of the spirit world. In some cultures, owls are often associated with death. As I researched animals spirits I discovered that owls are also linked with wisdom. And, (coincidentally), 'soph', the Greek root of Sofie's name, means wise.

Some Native American cultures believe owls represent the deceased and their newly released souls. Others believe that owls are messengers sent to collect the spirit. And some hold to the concept of 'shape-shifting', where an animal soul temporarily takes the physical form of a different animal to achieve a certain purpose.

Never since has it been as crisp and clear as it was that night, the conditions that allowed the illumination of Sofie to shine on. I have studied those treetops many times at dusk and, from the house, it is difficult to differentiate the individual tree crests, let alone the small form of an owl. And, had the owl not dipped low across the surface of the water, I would never have noticed it.

Whatever the true meaning might be, I found the experience comforting and a reminder that there is ample mystery in life that we may never know truth behind. But, we move forward and trust that the Universe is moving in a positive direction for the evolution of all.

The pain we feel when a good friend departs creates an opening for our next level of maturation and of understanding. Though we may feel like our lives have been shattered, we are sustained by the expansion and advancement that was fostered. And having known the wonder of such love leaves us more receptive to, in due course, take the risks involved in developing future relationships, or other endeavors which involve trust and courage. Eleven days after Sofie's departure, I was again meditating by the creek. And, as the passing of time does provide us with a broader perspective, I realize now, looking back, that was the day that Scotia was born:

Tonight, I was, again, sitting down by the creek. I had been there for around twenty minutes. It was becoming dark and I had in mind heading back to the house when I noticed, in the shades of dusk, a small otter swim by. Again, this is a life form I have never seen before on the creek. This animal delighted in darting through the water, totally capable of negotiating and reveling in the winter conditions. I thought, "There is an animal that won't drown." It had the qualities of another visit from Sofie, and it was calming to see her in her element, with no harm looming ahead. Even as a puppy, nosing young trout and splashing after birds and drifting leaves, she was an excellent swimmer. She was enthralled being in and around the water.

> *Some believe the otter represents balanced female energy. This joyful little creature is adventuresome, and assumes that all other creatures are friendly—until proven otherwise. Their energy creates space for others to enter their lives without preconceptions or suspicions. It is content to enjoy and share the good fortune of others. The otter transmits freedom of love without jealousy. It also represents women's healing wisdom: sensibility without suspicion, guidance in unmasking talents, psychic awareness, faithfulness and understanding the value of playtime.*[2]

> *This description fits Sofie's energy perfectly. May she swim freely with the flow of the Universe and never be afraid.*

Those days were also filled with an abiding concern for Sofie's soul. Having your vital, young life end so suddenly must have been a terrifying turn. Everything must stop, all that is familiar changing forms. It is the natural order when the deterioration of old age helps to prepare us for the departure from our body, when our bodily functions slowly cease to operate and our wishes and desires in the physical world begin to diminish. Nature readies us for this inevitable separation. But, as I pondered this unforeseen departure, abruptly thrust upon this young, vibrant life, I envisioned Sofie's anguish—that so many of her delights, her desires, would be left unfilled. Where do our dreams go when we die? I felt a tremendous, relentless fear of death, and after dark, at times, my body would actually tremble.

Eventually, I realized that I was sensing Sofie's final feelings in the physical world—of being alone, submersed in the dark waters—cold and dying. For several days I directed many thoughts to her; I imagined her surrounded with warmth and light, love and happiness. Over time, this sense of fear subsided and the shaking ceased. I continue to send her blessings every day, affirming that she is loved and remembered—that she will always be in my heart—that she is my inspiration.

Three months later, Sadie and I welcomed a new addition to the household. I desperately longed for a small dog, a loving spirit to hold and nurture, to share my love and adventure. And thus, Scotia O'Shea, another adventuresome, loving West Highland Terrier spirit, joined our household. Although no one would ever "replace" our beloved Sofie, Scotia brought her own brand of cheer to our lives.

Sadie had sorely missed her little friend. On each of our walks down by the creek where we found Sofie, Sadie would pause and stare, and, on at least two occasions, she tried to dig up Sofie's grave. Since my work takes me away from the house so much, I sensed that Sadie would enjoy another warm and loving presence to keep her company. From her first day in our home, Scotia adored Sadie; she was so full of vitality and spunk that Sadie didn't quite know how to react to this energetic white ball of fur. But, when I returned home, there they were, often lying next to each other—just as Sadie and Sofie had communed under the cottonwood shade tree— comforted that they faced life as a pack of two.

Spring is a time of renewal and rebirth, and so, it seemed fitting to add this fresh spirit to our lives. Four month later, during a hasty tour of the local farmer's market, the same dog breeder that I acquired Scotia from was there with an orphaned male Westie. He was small and stocky, and after five minutes, he stole my heart. And so, on a bright August morning, Dundee McDuff became the newest member of our growing pack.

Because of the shorter life span of dogs, we learn of death and all of its associated dimensions. Often, the first experience we have of death is the loss of a pet during our childhood. Shortly after Willis Morris left for college, Skip, the cherished dog of his boyhood, died. Skip was an old dog when Morris left for England, and he knew he would never see Skip again. A month later, he received a transatlantic call from his father telling him that Skip died. In his mourning he tells us, "The dog of your boyhood teaches you a great deal about friendship, and love, and death. Old Skip was my brother. They had buried him under our elm tree, they said—yet this was not totally true. For he really lay buried in my heart."[3]

Our grief, at these times, seems unbearable—often greater than we experience at the death of a human friend. This is a tribute to the purity and unselfishness of our dogs' gifts to us, their childlike innocence, vulnerability and trust. Dogs appear truly content only when they are engaged in relationships: with their human companions, other dogs, or their environment. This need is so dominant that they will exert enormous efforts to fulfill it. They are blessed with the capacity to fully engage in the present. They live so completely in the moment, in such rapture and authenticity, that we are often compelled to follow their example, to excavate our own true essence.

Dogs' pursuit of this bliss, through the thrills they seek, often costs them their lives. And the permanence of this change will, forever, transform the course of events. As Dylan Schaffer recounts the thoughts of Sixer, a dog watching from a nearby porch, of the imminent death of Carly, after she was struck by a car, "She knew, as I did, that the damage was serious and irreversible. Soon her owner would arrive, followed by a final trip to the vet. Carly's eyes told a hundred stories, of travels, of friends and rivals, of secret loves. She laughed at her recklessness and cursed the cold she now felt stretching through her once sturdy frame. Perhaps I should have gone to her. But I sat, motionless, savoring the sweet summer heat, waiting for the smell of mourning."[4]

Because they demonstrate love in such pure form, both giving and receiving, when a dog departs, a part of the intense grief we feel is that of our hearts missing their ability to reflect back to us our ability to give and receive love. This is such a vital need of the healthy human psyche that, when it is no longer available to us, the effects are profound. The death of a cherished pet can bring forth our most deep-seated fears and emotional conflicts. It may come in the form of a resurrection of unresolved grief from other losses in our lives, or perhaps as a stark and unyielding reminder of the mortality of all living things, including ourselves.

When Susan Chernak McElroy came to grips with the diagnosis of her own cancer, it was the memories of her beloved dog, Keesha, who had died from cancer, that gave her strength, "My worst fear was that I'd become hysterical and inconsolable at the end of my life. At that point, my only consolation was Keesha. In memory, I returned to that last day of ours over and over, not in terms of my pain but of her simple and elegant grace, and acceptance of her path."[5]

Milan Kundera describes a similar courage from Karenin, "Standing there watching him, they thought once more that he was smiling and that as long as he kept smiling he had a motive to keep living despite his death sentence."[6]

If we can remain open during this time of pain and loss, great emotional healing can occur. We learn that there are aspects of life that we cannot control, despite all our efforts. We learn the profound lessons of acceptance, that we are not perfect. We are forced to acknowledge our helplessness and to appreciate the full potential of each moment. By dedicating ourselves to being healed, we honor our departed friends' love and loyalty, knowing they would wish that for us.

When death is imminent, many dogs seek a solitary place to be by themselves. This might be hard for us to accept, but as James Thurber tells it in this stirring manner: "Death, to a dog, is the final unavoidable compulsion, the last ineluctable scent on a fearsome trail, but they like to face it alone, going out into the woods, among the leaves . . . enduring without sentimental human distraction the Last Loneliness, which they are wise enough to know cannot be shared by anyone."[7]

As much courage and devotion as our dogs display towards us, there are times we are called upon to be equally brave in making the choice for our gravely ill or dying pets: that of prolonged treatment versus euthanasia. This can be one of the most profoundly difficult choices we may ever face. The thought of choosing to assist our dogs in having a peaceful, loved-filled departure may, instead, be construed as killing them—betraying their trust, ending their lives prematurely. We may feel a desire to allow the animal to die naturally, even though the reality can mean protracted suffering or an exceedingly diminished quality of life. Ironically, euthanasia is not against the law for animals. In a society where they often have very limited rights, animals, unlike people in most states, have the right to a merciful death.

Montana winters can be brutal. When my beloved Cuya reached fourteen, her frail body, wracked with arthritis, drew my attention to this life/death dilemma. Her movements, once graceful and light were now tentative and measured. At times, I would let her outside to relieve herself and go out later, only to find her fallen on the frozen ground, unable to muster the strength to stand. Her once strong body was now unable to respond to her physical needs. She was almost deaf, her eyes glazed with cataracts.

This was my divine, vibrant friend who had climbed trees, vaulted onto her dog house and raced full speed into the wind. But, the most telling symptom was her waning interest in life, the joyful look in her eyes was replaced with a hollow, puzzled stare. And, like her father, Scruff, so many years before, Cuya's days were endured rather than embraced. When I would return home, she scarcely acknowledged my entry and then, only with a slight turn of her head. I knew in my heart that she was ready to move on, to release her spent body so that her spirit could soar, liberated and unfettered.

Winter approached with the reality that Cuya would again struggle with daily life and the brutal effects the cold climate wrecked on her weak, fragile body. And so, with a laden heart, I made the decision to help her on her final journey. We spent our last day together visiting her favorite places, indulging her with her favorite treats. But, finally the time came to make our one last voyage together. An extraneous force took me through the motions. Ever obedient, Cuya climbed onto the backseat of my car for her own final trip to the vet.

I could not believe the foreign reality that I faced and what it would mean for both of us. Cuya had been my finest friend for fourteen years—kindred sister spirits, we had shared the prime of our lives together. I envisioned a future alone, and where would she be? Endless doubts shadowed my senses. Could I possibly handle this—the unthinkable? Was this the correct course for her, for us both? There were no answers, only questions and a forbidding burden, oppressive in my heart. But, I realized what had to be done, as one friend helping another.

The veterinarian and his assistant are evolving saints if their concerns and actions that day were any indication of their normal routine. We all gathered close by Cuya, stroking her gently, softly, offering words of comfort and assurance. She accepted this kind treatment, but seemed to sense that something momentous was about to happen. Yet, she did not struggle or resist as the veterinarian administered an injection to induce unconsciousness. After Cuya entered this peaceful state, he gave her the second injection, the one that would stop her heart. I knew there was no going back. Our gentle words and compassionate, soothing caresses continued as we waited, and even in her state of unconsciousness, when this drug took effect, she gave one last tremor; her will to live was so great.

I left through the back door into a blustery, gray November day, my eyes, my life, blurred in a veil of tears, each breath a labored ordeal. At that moment, the cosmic distance between this world and the next seemed ethereal, the journey smothering and dark.

The grief lasted for weeks, months, and even now, more than ten years later, the memory of that day stops everything, as I pause and thank Cuya for the sublime dignity she brought to my life. A few weeks after her death, I visited an astute friend and related the agony of the decision— that I still anguished over whether I had made the correct choice. Had I betrayed Cuya's trust; did I fail her? This wise confidante dismissed my fears and guilt. She told me that, yes, Cuya and I had forged a very strong bond of trust, and Cuya had trusted me—enough to know that when the time came, I would be there to help her through this most important transition. I absolutely believe that her spirit still soars, that her unique life power and her presence are still a vital force in the Universe. And, as I accepted her physical death, I sensed that her transformation was certain. The perfect cycle seemed complete. There was no death, only love and life.

As Gary Kowalski counsels about euthanasia, "When it is a compassionate response to suffering, it can become a source of wisdom and a door for growth."[8] If we can allow the pain of such intense grief to open our hearts, we open our souls to be touched, and through the death experience, we embrace the possibility for new life and re-birth. Our departed loved ones would never wish grief upon us. Often we feel the comfort of their love, even after they have passed out of this world. In the words of Eckhart, "Life dies but being goes on." Perhaps the spirits of our departed friends seek to ease our pain, to bolster our own odyssey, just as they did when they were physically present in our lives.

Rituals can help us deal with this profound transition. Carefully tending to the body, preparing a special burial site, and permitting our close friends to share and participate can be powerful and healing. Writing a poem, a song or a letter can help clarify the many remarkable gifts we shared and help keep them alive in our hearts. Or read a verse that has special significance:

> *. . .When thou takest away their breath, they fail*
> *And they return to the dust from which they came;*
> *but when thou breathest into them, they recover;*
> *Thou givest new life to the earth.*
>
> *—Psalm 104*

I had Cuya's earthly remains cremated and kept the ashes for many years, until I could place them in a special place of honor. She is buried on the creek bank where Sofie and I shared so many memorable moments. I created a small flower garden surrounding a curly willow tree and four quaking aspens. A small terra cotta statue of Saint Francis was recently added, affirming his ardent love for animals.

Across the creek lies Sofie's sanctuary. It overlooks the place of her departure, where each day the soft winds move towards the setting sun. I added a young evergreen tree to the mature row of fir trees—the trees where the owl waited. And a mound of river rocks firmly secures the spot, just as she remains resolutely bound to my heart.

In his moving book *Colter*, Rick Bass recalls his prolonged search, and the eventual discovery of the body of his beloved dog, Colter, who was killed by an unknown assailant. He remembers, "I buried him with shells, both 12- and 20-gauge, for whenever we went hunting again, and I put in extras because I knew I'd miss some shots. The bones of his quarry. A whistle, a brass bell. Then, the earth back in over him, and new grief in over old grief, like a mountain eroding to bury with its disintegrating sediments, disintegrating heart and body, something bright and valuable below."[9] His haunting advice is both moving and wise counsel, "You never know when the last hunt is going to be."[10]

In Marjorie Garber's remarkable book *Dog Love*, she shares the words of columnist Anna Quindlen, after the passing of her dog, Jason Oliver C. Smith, ". . . He never bit anyone, which is more than you can say for most of us."[11] Dog love brings so much into our lives, as Garber believes, "'More than you can say for most of us' is, in a way, the perfect canine epitaph."[12]

We all experience grief and pain. By sharing our feelings we can help heal others.

By revealing our stories, we may open the door for others to do the same. And ultimately the realization of the joys and love we have experienced helps us through this *painful time of loss. It is the sense of **love** that lives on forever and enriches our lives.*

By immersing ourselves in the depths of grief, we are cleansed and healed. We learn that each life and each death is significant.

By developing a reverence for life, we are better prepared for the road ahead as we honor each soul.

By feeling the constancy of love, our lives are connected in this most amazing bond, and we are given a more solid direction into the future.

If we fail to live fully, we increase our fear of loss and death—the void of what we lack. Sofie so bravely and enthusiastically faced each day, each adventure, that her life, while short in years, was infinite in evolution and happiness. She was a superb example of a living force, of one who loved life intimately, thoroughly, and she assigned that special gift to the world around her. Sofie believed in life and lived that belief. All that we embraced and shared became a part of her soul and mine—a mystical, eternal bond that will never die.

Uncover the priceless rarity of each moment. Do not postpone conferring your attention to the essential, true moments of substance. Change is always with us; so we never know when the form of something rare and precious could be forever altered, with no chance to prepare or to say farewell.

Birth and Death: could any of us invent a more beautiful way to enter this world or devise a more natural route for leaving it at the end? Animals enrich our lives in countless ways, with their playfulness, their tranquility, their constancy, and their love. If they can help us remember that death is not our enemy, but simply one more moment in the world's endless process of becoming, dissolution, and renewal, they will have imparted a final gift.[13]

—Gary Kowalski

Chapter 11

LOYALTY AND GRATITUDE

Dogs. They are better than human beings because they know but they do not tell.
> —Emily Dickinson, poet and recluse (1830-1886)

Histories are more full of examples of the fidelity of dog than of friends.
> —Alexander Pope, English poet (1688-1744)

Regardless of the circumstances, dogs remain steadfast, unwavering in their true calling—to share love and remain loyal. This solid base guides their actions with clarity and resolution. Dogs do, substantially, *live* their inner truths. These inherent values are deeply-seated in their temperaments. They have no need to contemplate endlessly, fret, or get "another opinion," as humans are so prone to do. Dogs intuitively track the correct course. Their paths blend love, loyalty, and trust with their heart as navigator. Again, is it any wonder they remind us of angels?

Their spontaneous expressions lack fear and indecision. This allows them to engage fully in life-affirming relationships as they integrate the rhythm of life with the steady loyalty that lies fixed in their nature. One of the most famous accounts of a dog's loyalty towards his master is the story of Greyfriar's Bobby. His actions are legendary throughout Scotland—so celebrated are they, that the town of Edinburgh erected a statue in his honor that sits on Candlemaker's Row above a granite fountain created for dogs.

In 1858, Bobby, a young Skye terrier, lost his master, Auld Jock. According to the legend, Bobby followed the group of mourners to the church, and, after the services were over and everyone had left, the grief-stricken little dog laid down on his master's grave. He remained there for fourteen years, sleeping by the tombstone each night until his own death in 1872. Concerned individuals brought him food and water over the years, but regardless of the weather, he remained there. After his death, a special exception was made so he could be buried next to his master. Bobby holds a special place of pride in the hearts of Scots, and his actions could not have paid a higher, more loving tribute to the life and deeds of his master.

Thousands of miles away and nearly a century later, Montana's Hi-Line region, the northernmost railroad route near the Canadian border, produced its own version of a dog's unquestioning love and devotion for his master. Shep was a collie-cross dog who belonged to a Fort Benton sheep herder. When the old man died, his friends took his body to the train station (back when it used to run through Fort Benton). Shep somberly followed his master's casket and watched as it was loaded onto the train. From that day on, until his death some five years later, Shep never left the tracks. He greeted every incoming train, looking for his master—waiting for him to return.

At first, the station crew wondered where this dog (who greeted every train) had come from. Eventually, they pieced the story together. Some of them attempted to entice Shep home with them, but he refused to leave the tracks. Finally the station employees acquiesced to Shep's desires, and fed him and cared for him by the tracks. Years later, old and nearly blind, Shep was run over by one of the incoming trains. Saddened by this tragic end to Shep's engrossing saga, the citizens of Fort Benton buried him on a hill above the train station; symbolically he would always overlook the tracks. At Shep's funeral, hundreds of mourners gathered to pay tribute to this devoutly loyal dog, while a solitary Boy Scout played Taps.

In the summer of 1994, the citizens of Fort Benton raised enough money to commission a bronze statue dedicated to Shep. The monument, a hearty looking, larger than life-sized dog, is erected in the heart of Fort Benton, a park that faces the Victorian Grand Union Hotel on the shores of the Missouri River. The statue was created by artist Bob Scriver, and cost $120,000—a veritable fortune by small town Montana standards. Shep has been venerated as the world's most faithful dog, and he remains a Hi-Line legend. Shep's unceasing devotion to his master touched the hearts of many. It is encouraging that such a lifetime of hallowed dedication was recognized and honored; that this low-keyed, hard working farming community paid tribute to his virtues, and, that Shep's memory and commitment to his master will be preserved as an exemplification for future generations.

Through their own humble, honest actions, dogs demonstrate how to embrace what we love and cultivate who we are—to act on our inner wisdom and foster this vision as a priority in our lives. Because dogs accept us lovingly, without censor, they help us to uncover our higher selves. They steadfastly demonstrate the importance of forgiveness, and we realize, from their lack of malice, the healing and nurturing effects this state of grace has on our energy. Dogs will remain with us, through good times and bad, and their open humility and trust guide us towards having more faith in ourselves—in Life. In essence, dogs display the courage and stoicism to face the world at large.

With openness and humility, dogs endow us with the greatest gift on earth, *love*. And they do so, regardless of what they receive in return. The bounds of their hearts know no limits. What an amazing accomplishment! Jesus, Ghandi, Mother Theresa, the Dalai Lama, and other exalted world leaders have had this ability. Their capacity to soothe and befriend, in this matter, have made them legends, saints— God made manifest on earth. It is clear that the human race is greatly in need of such examples of courage, wisdom, loyalty, and love. Dogs serve as our gentle reminders. Hopefully, we can offer our own contributions to acknowledge and reciprocate these fine qualities.

So, in keeping with this wisdom, be kind to yourself, and to those around you, including your loyal pets. Honor your feelings, and resolve to adjust any areas of your life that may cause harm. Develop a sense of *loyalty* to goodness, a commitment to strive for what is in the best interest of all. We all make mistakes; so, it is important to learn from them, knowing you did the best you could do at the time and then move on.

Acknowledge your accomplishments, and practice the belief that you *can* have such success routinely. Be actively involved in your life's routine; engage with your environment and humankind in the broad arena. Take time to reflect when that is appropriate, and conversely, take action, when involvement is germane to the situation. As you mature and expand from your daily affairs, notice how you become filled with a solid bounty, richer, fuller—more at peace.

Little Sofie made advances through each of her adventures. Occasionally, her acts of daring would result in "crash and burn" consequences. But, she was a rapid learner; she rarely repeated her mistakes, and those endeavors that were successful, propelled her on to even grander challenges. Despite her rather diminutive stature, Sofie presented a confident, positive persona. Other dogs, and the people she encountered, seemed to sense her spunk and regarded her in a way that, in turn, reinforced her self confidence—her ease with the world. This translated into Sofie demonstrating for others her delightful quest to find joy in life, to make the very most of each moment.

Most dogs, by their very natures, have gentle, loving souls. They generously impart their allegiance in a convivial, compassionate manner. Sometimes, it seems as if they simply cannot extend their devotion enough. Their affection inspires a like response in others, as they assist and support us in discovering our personal strengths and heartfelt truths. The loyal bond they form with their human companions is evident when we take them for a walk that involves encounters with other dogs. Initially, when they meet the other dogs, their joy and instant camaraderie seem to know no limits. They capitalize on this instant species recognition and squeeze a macrocosm of emotional and physical excitement into these short, intense interactions. But, when it is time to depart, and they are called to accompany us, dogs will leave their new friends, seemingly without a second thought. If they become accidentally separated from their human companions, the concern and panic evident on their faces is quite genuine—like a child separated from its parent. Dogs exude a sense of "pack loyalty," a longing for a place with which they identify—a place associated with their exchanges of love, of comfort and happiness.

Konrad Lorenz delineated between "aureus dogs" and "wolf dogs" when he suggested that canine breeds that demonstrate friendliness towards everyone are descended from the jackal (Canis aureus). Those breeds that bonded with only one master descended from the wolf (Canis lupus). In Lorenz's estimation, the "jackal-dog" appeared juvenile and acquiescent, responding towards his master as a combination of parent and god. The "wolf dog" showed neither of these tendencies and responded to his master more as an equal. It establishes a bond that is stronger and less transferable to another person. It is clear that the wolf dog possessed the temperament that Lorenz found preferable.[1]

There are accounts of the loyalty of dogs that date as far back as the eight century B.C., when Homer told of his faithful hound, Argos, in the *Odyssey*. While Odysseus was away for twenty years, involved in the Trojan War, Argos waited patiently for his return. Odysseus finally returned, in disguise, to avoid the men plotting to kill him. Argos recognized him and wagged his tail. But, even though the dog had waited two decades for his return, Odysseus could not acknowledge his beloved dog without endangering his own life. Homer relates how Odysseus wept in grief when Argos, neglected and incapacitated, lowered his head for the final time onto the pile of excrement where he had been stationed and died.

Napoleon underwent a profound revelation after the Battle of Bassano, during his Italian campaign. He had long resented the attention that his wife showered upon her small dog. This contempt developed into a disregard for dogs in general. He chained dogs along the walls of Alexandria, Egypt to furnish warnings of approaching enemies. He believed the presence of the dogs would slow advancing invaders, and he cared little if a few dogs were sacrificed in the process.

On the night following the battle, as he walked across the battlefield covered with corpses, he came upon this scene, which he dictated to his secretary Emmanuel, the Comte de Las Cases in 1815:

> *We were alone, in the deep solitude of a beautiful moonlit night. Suddenly a dog leaped out from under the cloak of a corpse. He came running toward us and then, almost immediately afterward ran back to his dead master, howling piteously. He licked the soldier's unfeeling face, then ran back to us—repeating this several times. He was seeking both help and revenge. I don't know whether it was the mood of the moment, or the place, or the time, or the action in itself, or what—at any rate, it's a fact that nothing I saw on any other battlefield ever produced a like impression on me. I stopped involuntarily to contemplate this spectacle. This man, I said to myself, had friends, perhaps. He may have some at camp, in his company—and here he lies, abandoned by all except his dog. What a lesson nature was teaching us through an animal.*

> *What a strange thing is man! How mysterious are the workings of his sensibility! I had commanded in battles that were to decide the fate of a whole army and felt no emotion. I had watched the execution of manoeuvers that were bound to cost the lives of many among us, and my eyes remained dry. And suddenly I was shaken, turned inside out, by a dog howling in pain!*

Perhaps, this scene had added impact, since, only a few months earlier, Napoleon's own life had been saved by a dog. In February, 1815, he decided to end his self-imposed exile on the island of Elba. As his boat pulled away, he stood near the gunwale, taking in one last view of the island. The sea was rough and pitched the boat about, soaking the decks. After a short time, Napoleon turned up missing; he had lost his balance and was thrown into the water. Unable to swim, he struggled in the water until a large black and white Newfoundland came to his rescue. The dog belonged to a fisherman and helped tow lines to small boats and retrieve fishing nets. He swam to the fallen general and kept his head above water until the boat returned to rescue Napoleon. After the rescue, Napoleon proclaimed, "Here, Gentlemen, a dog teaches us a lesson in humanity."

The courageous dog's name is unknown. It is presumed that he was reunited safely with the fisherman. Regardless of the fact that his rescue target was a famous man who held dogs in great contempt, this kind creature followed his natural inclinations and helped Napoleon live to experience another momentous event—his defeat at Waterloo.

As dogs give us unconditional love and compassion from the depths of their souls, they assist us in being able to follow their example. Dogs don't cloud their mission with doubt and mental debate. Their astounding faculties propel them into the future, but they act in the now and are instantly rewarded in the present. We, too, can do the same.

It is feasible to heal past wounds and create a better future, but we must undertake this endeavor in the present. If we practice holding love in our hearts, in all that we say and do, it is conceivable to redeem many past actions of distrust, envy, hatred and anger. The river of our lives will flow more freely, as we broadcast these gentle and kindly thoughts. By advancing from a perspective of love, we expand from within, and draw to us, more constructive notice, and thus, enhance our engagement with others.

Humankind has always possessed this innate ability, but somewhere along the winding course of evolution, many of us have derailed from the 'love train.' Most likely it resulted from our propensity to forge through life, relying primarily on the appraisal of our minds, and relegating our senses and emotions to a secondary role. Or, perhaps it came from a feeling of betrayal by someone in our past, thus rendering us unable to move beyond this hurt to a renewed state of trust. Unfortunately, these limited, compromised perspectives stifle a great deal of our potential and prevent our capabilities from being discovered, developed and fulfilled. Such a narrow, less than fully dimensional approach, can yield a shallow and frustrating journey through life.

Be thankful for the love and all other precious elements in your life and they will multiply. The Universe manifests what we center our attention on, so it pays to acknowledge the good in your life if you want it to continue or increase. As Eckhart teaches: if you feel inclined to pray, but are not sure what to say; "Thank you" will always suffice.

Extend gratitude to your dogs and other sources of love in your life if you want this supportive bounty to endure. And, in turn, offer your own loyalty towards these benefactors to complete this circle of trust. This reciprocal state of mutual regard restores your emotional well-being and expedites the manifestation of your deepest desires.

Henry Suso, a contemporary and student of Eckhart's, described the profound intimacy of this state of loyalty in his *Little Book of Wisdom*, "To be a stranger to Thee for one day is a thousand years to a loving heart."[2] The Universe, the Force of Origination, receives your requests; however, the answers may present themselves in unexpected forms. There is a greater creative energy force available than we may realize, if only we are open to receive it. The love we invite can expose in us a state of peace and relaxation and allow us to rejuvenate, to create a space for our higher good. The inner peace that dogs achieve may have its roots in their autonomy from needing specific results. They persevere and create a state of common good, regardless of the response. They continue to give selflessly, radiating their benevolence and generosity with an honest and accepting heart— exuding these admirable traits to the end.

Emotions guide the life's journey of dogs. As much as they give and love, they also experience profound grief when they are separated from those they love. Throughout my life, I have taken trips where my dogs were unable to go along. Upon my return, without fail, I received reports from their care-givers of the dogs moping about for days, profoundly downhearted, not responding to diversions that were offered.

For at least a year after Sofie died, whenever Sadie and I walked down to the creek, she always went directly to the spot where I retrieved Sofie's body, and during the summer, she wore a path in the grass from these daily pilgrimages. She would gaze at the water, adrift in her own private reverie, and, after a few minutes, would turn and gaze at me, as if expecting an answer—an explanation I could not provide.

Dogs, in essence, *are* love, loyalty and devotion, and, it is for these reasons, that we are drawn to them in such a compelling manner. We feel affirmed and strengthened by them. Their gentle, curious, healing energy touches our souls (not to mention our bedroom slippers), and we are richer for the experience. As we learn to project such positive energy into our lives and relationships, all that we contact will advance, as we co-create an enhanced haven for all of Creation.

> *I could not go away from Miss Laura, even to die. When my last hour comes, I want to see her gentle face bending over me, and then I shall not mind how much I suffer.[3]*
> —Marshall Saunders, *Beautiful Joe*

> *There is no faith which has never yet been broken, except that of a truly faithful dog.*
> —Konrad Z. Lorenz, Austrian naturalist (1903-1989)

Chapter 12

HIGHER AWARENESS

*When we look into the eyes of an angel animal, we see their
spiritual Natures. We see ourselves reflected in their gentle
gaze. We see the work of a loving God.*[1]

—Allen and Linda Anderson

*So my dog is a sort of guru. When I become too serious and
preoccupied, he reminds me of the importance of frolicking
and play. When I get too wrapped up in abstractions and
ideas, he reminds me of the importance of exercising and caring for my body. On his own canine level, he shows me that
it might be possible to live without inner conflicts or neu-
roses: uncomplicated, genuine and glad to be alive.*[2]

—Gary Kowalski

During the early years of my childhood, it was an inexplicably
serene occasion to visit Miss Brown. Whenever our family dropped by
to see our neighbors at the George ranch, it was their collie-cross dog,
Miss Brown, who, with gracious decorum, presided over the visit.
From my youthful perspective as a rambunctious tomboy, I was drawn
to the dramatic forces of nature and the calming comfort of the animal
world. Greeting our fellow ranchers was secondary, although the
George family did intimate Miss Brown in temperament and cordiali-
ty. As we drove up their lane, I faithfully watched for Miss Brown—

always at her primary station near the house, lying under a huge weeping willow tree at the edge of their Arabian horse pasture. From her chosen post, she had a clear view of everything significant within her domain: cattle, horses, storms and approaching guests. Her gentle, welcoming presence seemed to invite a personal exchange with any visitors before the business of human socializing began.

Miss Brown bore a striking resemblance to my own beloved dog, Mister, which endeared her to me even more. As she slowed with age, it seemed even more respectful to pay her homage at her appointed post. She projected an essence of kind regard, welcoming and accepting— the qualities we should, perhaps, seek to emulate ourselves, and revere more in others.

The kind and tender affirmations that dogs bestow link us effortlessly with our innate requirements for spiritual advancement and emotional validation. By their example, we gain a fundamental moral perception, a commitment to explore the vast mystery of our place in the universal setting.

Our mystical dog friends demonstrate how to utilize and expand our intuition, our creativity, and set a course in the world, however humble it may appear. We become one with our path. As Brian Vesey-Fitzgerals shares:

> *The dog has an absolutely uncanny knack of knowing what we are thinking, even of what we are feeling . . . but I do not really understand my dogs. Many and many a time I have been aware that they have been trying to tell me something. But I am unable to cross the frontier into the dog's mind. They, it seems to me, can cross the frontier into my mind whenever they wish. The fact is that the dog can live, happily and at ease, in two worlds: his own and our own. We can live only in our own. They are cleverer than we are.[3]*

The cornerstone for most spiritually seeking individuals is the belief that we have souls—that the soul is the underlying essence of life, the depth of our abilities to experience feelings as sentient beings. Carl Jung described the soul as being partly in eternity and partly in time. Soul is present whenever our lives intersect the dimension of the holy: in moments of intimacy, in flights of fancy, and in rituals that hallow the evanescent events of our lives with enduring significance. At some level, our souls are a reflection of the whole.

Is it possible to say for certain which life-forms possess souls? This question has been debated for centuries and is not one that can be resolved with empirical evidence. Perhaps, each of us must solve this enigma individually, by opening our hearts beyond what we know. When asked the question, "Do dogs have souls?" for those who cherish and revere dogs for their dignity, their loyalty and love, their ability to experience joy and withstand suffering—to inspire and promote harmony—the answer is a resounding, "Yes!" Souls do not belong to humans alone. The Latin root for soul, "anima," also belongs to the word animal. The soul is that which gives life.

When we recognize and celebrate the sacredness in all life forms, we come to understand that God, the Originator, is a part of all creation. This creative force approaches the incomprehensible—perfect and beyond limitation. It forms us, nurtures and comforts us. It inspires and heals us, and, it is freely available—this potency that makes us whole. The great mystics believe that soul is delivered through living and enduring. So by navigating the life-scape of joy, grief, and healing, compassion is born.

Discovering and imparting compassion and sensitivity is a critical part of the spiritual journey. It heals our wounds and uncovers our core, authentic nature. Eckhart says that the soul grows by subtraction, through sorrow and suffering. It can also evolve through praise and openness. He believes that, to truly know what the soul is would require supernatural knowledge. It is indescribable, transcendent. This awareness must come from grace, for the soul is where God works compassion.

All of these boundless, ineffable qualities are a part and substance of our beloved animal friend, the dog. Instead of acting as humans do, dogs come from their own unique perspective. Border collies have been credited with having a mystical ability to read the minds of their human companions. They respond to a vast number of commands, often at great distance. The connection they have, that allows them to intuit the desires of their human partners, is exceptional. Their ability to interpret and to react is uncommon, unequivocally remarkable. As a novice in a local agility class, Scotia (and I) enjoyed the irrepressible enthusiasm of several border collies. Their human trainers did their best to act as if they were in charge, but ultimately, these spirited dogs left us all in the dust.

A part of mysticism is trusting our experiences, knowing when to take action, or when to refrain, when to give, and when to receive. Dogs often prefer the company of humans to that of other dogs, and, at times, they may appear to love us more than we are capable of loving others— or even ourselves. Thus, their mystical qualities reach out to touch us and reveal alternative, more preferable ways of conducting our affairs. Dogs can unmask our finest qualities and encourage us to reach even higher. Italian dog expert, Piero Scanziani, who created the motto: "Let us demonstrate that man knows how to defend a friend,"[4] believes that a dog has a soul as surely as it has a body. He believes that the soul of a dog is immensely rich because of the many deeply felt emotions that dogs experience.

Years ago I embarked on a substantial day hike through the Mission Mountains, near Flathead Lake in western Montana. My destination was the Mud Lakes, a series of four increasingly higher alpine lakes, hidden in the dense forestation of the Mission Mountains. My beloved Old English Sheepdog matriarch, Cuya, and her son, Little Bear, kept me company with diligence and enthusiasm. It was a blistering summer day, and the trail seemed almost vertical at certain stages. We crawled through the dense underbrush and clutched bushes and roots to gain leverage and maintain any momentum. The exertion of energy was tremendous; our fortitude and resolve were sorely tested.

One phase of the ascent compelled us to cross a sheer shale face, with the evidence of many avalanches strewn and shattered below. As we inched our way across the narrow jagged ledge, the dogs and I stayed within reach of each another, one ahead and one aft. For most of the way, we comprised a dog/human/dog sandwich, determined to prove that there is safety in numbers. Or, was it that insanity is contagious? Regardless, we all sensed the danger.

As I negotiated a tight squeeze around an out-hanging boulder, I stopped and gripped the massive rock to steady my balance, trailing Cuya and Little Bear who had already passed around it. Suddenly, the entire boulder came loose in front of me and crashed between my feet before hurling its way down the slope. Cuya and Little Bear watched in astonishment and trepidation. We all froze, incredulous at the dramatic event, knowing that any one of us could have easily been the crashing object of descent, instead of the huge stone.

After the boulder slammed into its resting place and the dust began to settle, we slowly and somberly finished the traverse. It seemed like an eternity, but finally we felt the firm forest floor beneath our feet. The shale was conquered. Onward to the lakes. We were triumphant! Once again, the hike became a lively adventure. We had encountered an extreme challenge and emerged victoriously. Our fearless trio overcame anxiety, and remained calm, against great odds. We managed to extricate ourselves from danger, with only a twinge of panic and no physical harm. Our nerve trauma was quickly forgotten. We were heroes, if only to ourselves. Quite a feat for three rough and tumble dare-devils. But, each success makes future tests all the more enticing. Mastery and victory, confidence and realization, all build on prior accomplishments, and raise the stakes for future achievements.

Eventually, around mid-day, we reached the shores of the fourth and final lake. Huge, flat rock formations, washed clean by the wind, covered most of the lake-side area. Forest sediment and conifer twigs laced our hair and clods of the timberland floor coated our feet. Alpine birds sounded their alerts, curious and vigilant about our foreign presence. Sweltering and exhausted, but satisfied with our conquest, our stamina was acutely depleted. We were spent, weak from the exertion of the climb, and faint from the summer heat. So, right there, in the middle of a sultry summer day, we all three lay down on a massive rock and drifted soundly asleep. That mid-day nap is the only occasion in my life that I have slept on a rock in the full sunlight, but I do not recall ever having a more satisfying rest. And, the fact that the dogs kept me company, dozing by my side, rather than seeking shade as they might normally do, attested to the depth of our common achievement, our mutual desire to continue the experience together.

A state of relaxation and focus helped us face our fears. Cuya, Little Bear, and I willed ourselves to be vulnerable, to let the natural course of events unfold. We conquered an extreme challenge and discovered pristine sensations, fresh solutions to problems that connected us with higher aspirations. We waited until late in the afternoon to descend. Refreshed by the cooler air, buoyed and rested, we had even more reason to believe in our capabilities, as we celebrated our success—*together*.

Dogs provide attendant support and good spirits as we make this important journey of self-discovery. Because it can be, for some, a lifelong voyage, our companion teachers will change along the way. But, the guidance we require will present itself in the most perfect form available, if we are able to remain aware—to recognize and accept help, and even *ask* for it. When a phase is completed, it may be necessary to release that teacher with love and gratitude and look to the future for the next open door that beacons to us.

Remember the times you have achieved inner peace? When you intended, with great purpose, to create more? Spending time in the company of a dog provides us endless examples of this state of generation and helps us recreate this experience in the outer world. Marjorie Garber believes that adults as well as children anthropomorphize (ascribe human characteristics to non-human things) dogs to regain their sense of collective human experience. That, paradoxically, the quintessence of the "human" is often found in the dog.[5] If this frame of reference is helpful, we can actively choose to operate on this level and accept nothing less.

As I sat and wrote these words by the flowing water, one bird began its spring time trilling. In a matter of minutes, the trees were filled with wrens and chickadees, boisterously playing—dislodging chunks of snow from the branches above onto my writing pad. Our muskrat swimming mentor paddled by, directly towards the rising sun, resolute in her mission.

Like Sofie, and all my dog friends have shown me, our experiences reflect our beliefs. When I am inspired to seek vivacity and beauty, I find it ever present around me. Infinitely grateful for the abundance of animals in my life, I treasure and revere them for the divine blessings they bestow. Living in Montana increases my chances for these hallowed encounters, but the majesty of life exists everywhere.

Dogs, in their authentic state, teach us to remain steadfast to our inner truths, to accept ourselves and the world around us, as it is, and to defend these truths. Growth and change can proceed from this point, but if, instead, we resist and remain focused on limitations or scarcity, the ascent we face towards actualization will be much steeper.

As you seek to make improvements in your life, begin by clarifying the essence of what you want. Be *specific* about your desires, but be open to the endless forms in which they may manifest. *Know*, as your dog friends bear witness, that you need very little to be truly happy. For many dogs, sharing time with their human companions seems to be the ultimate, satisfying experience, and they will go to great lengths to achieve it.

Sofie spent her last two Independence Day holidays and her final New Year's Eve celebration perched contentedly on my lap, in rapture, watching the fireworks displays off in the distance. She took immense interest in the blazing spectacles, and stayed with me, patiently, into the wee hours of a new millennium, a time for a new start both literally and figuratively. Sadly, it was only eleven days into the new year of 2000 that she left this world and began a new adventure in another dimension. Sofie was always there for me—whether it was a momentous event, surviving a trying time, or just sitting with me, sharing the evening sundown. Her sweet face gave me such delight and hope that each day, as a thank you, I send those loving sentiments back to her and all my departed canine friends.

Dogs, by sharing these modest but essential pleasures in our lives, in their natural, easy manner, solidify a place in our hearts and lives. They become a vital member of our *family*, and countless proud individuals carry pictures of their dogs in their wallets. It is estimated that dogs are named in the wills of at least one million Americans. Dogs are an integral, indispensable component of many human lives and with good reason. They sense our needs and desires and, in their humble, loving manner, weave a delightful element into our life experience.

As we develop the ability to express our feelings, freely, naturally, and authentically, we discover our true selves: warts, halos and everything in between. As Scottish author Sir Walter Scott tells us, "Recollect that the Almighty who gave the dog to be companion of our pleasures and our toils, hath invested in him with a nature noble and incapable of deceit." By observing these commendable traits, we may choose to raise the bar on our own efforts and conduct. As we travel this path, seeking sincerity and honor, we begin to feel stronger, more noble—truer to ourselves and others. We move beyond self-absorption. We see the benefits of sacrifice. We appreciate the ability to set aside the pressures of social conditioning, vanity and selfishness. We discover the benefits of taking risks, believing we can be powerful and reliable—a force of truth and love in the world. We can begin by practicing, as dogs do, the silence and simplicity that allows our greater core truths to be heard.

Dogs pursue the divine mystery of each moment with grand intent and enthusiastic participation. This feeds their souls and fulfills their passion. Skip enriched Willie Morris' boyhood in countless ways. It seemed that, in addition to being his constant and loyal companion, Skip also had political opinions that he endeavored to share. In that era, news of World War 11 was delivered into the average American home through radio broadcasts. Skip, upon hearing Hitler's burning words and shouts, "would sit there for a moment imbibing this bombast, then with his ears twitching as in pain, begin strutting about the room emitting deranged little howls, his snout lifted mightily upward, much as he had done in the cemetery when we accosted the man making the shortcut. Often was the time we had to turn off the radio to get him to stop. Why did he never once do this when listening to Mussolini? Was this a part of his ESP in reading my own moods about matters? Whatever it was, I never knew a dog so down on Hitler."[6]

We, too, may encounter similar circumstances, and it is the illumination of our unique perspective that puts our own personal spin on our experience of reality. Embrace and celebrate your uniquely defined presence in the world, and those beliefs will sustain and define you. Discover your paradise—the courage to live fully. Each moment is a miracle. Nurture it; develop it; make it the finest it can be, so that at the end of life's journey, you can look back with satisfaction and move forward without regrets.

In that frigid January nighttide, I kept my vigil, remembering Sofie, holding close her valor, her spirit—watching, waiting, and suddenly the owl appeared. The feathered benefactor provided comfort and mystery, a conundrum—but no revelation. I still endeavor to decipher the message. But it seems we are only destined to know the answers to certain questions. The rest of our journey is an enigma to embrace and abide.

The greatness of a nation and its moral progress can be measured by the way in which its animals are treated.
—Mahatma Gandhi

All knowledge, the totality of all questions and answers, is contained in the dog.

—Franz Kafka, Czech author (1883-1924)

Chapter 13

COURAGE AND PROTECTION

Beneath this spot are deposited the remains of a being who was possessed of Beauty without Vanity, Strength without Insolence, Courage without Ferocity, and all the Virtues of Man, without his Vices.
[Inscription on the monument to Boatswain, Lord Byron's beloved Newfoundland dog. The quote is often attributed to Byron, but was actually penned by his friend Hobhouse.]
—John Cam Hobhouse, British statesman (1786-1732)

Because their actions are so undeniably authentic, dogs can inspire humans to express our own core truths and the emotions that guide us. Countless dogs have risked their lives to save others, with no thought for their own safety. They live this truth, and, perhaps, they can inspire us to develop our own courage to face life's challenges.

In the early 1980's, during my time on Flathead Lake, I faced many hair-raising escapades in the company of my courageous Old English Sheepdog, Cuya. More than once, these ventures produced potentially life and death consequences.

Cuya gave birth to her only litter of puppies when she was three. Their entrance into the world was a much anticipated event, and, as soon as she delivered the first pup, I called my workplace to say I would be out for the rest of the day. The office had, of course, been updated throughout their nine week gestation period, and the staff knew that the pups were on their way. My co-workers also knew how deeply concerned and excited I was for this momentous event in Cuya's young life.

The pups came into the world, as expected, about one every hour. I toweled them dry, removed the mucous plugs from their mouths to ensure proper breathing, and then carefully placed them back in their bed under the watchful eye of their devoted mother. Cuya whelped eight puppies in total; unfortunately the smallest one lived only a week. He labored for a space to nurse, but, even with extra attention, he did not survive. Our vet said that often the very small pups have underdeveloped organs that ultimately contribute to their deaths. We grieved for his short life and buried him under a lilac tree, symbolically, for shade and protection.

When the pups were about twelve weeks old they each weighed around twenty pounds and were vigorous and spirited beyond anything you see in dog food commercials. Even our twice daily walks to the lake, down through the park, did not satiate their desire to roam and frolic. So, early one spring day, I loaded the entire family in my tired old '51 Gimmy pickup and drove to the countryside to let them run on the south shore where I had lived with Scruff and Cuya years before. I had in mind an ideal trail that wove through the woods where I had cross country skied and rode horseback. It was perfect.

We rattled up the road—the pups packed into the cab, panting and whimpering, each one vying for the best view on their first trip to the country. Cuya navigated from the truck box, reveling in all the details of the place where she, herself, spent her first year as a puppy. At last, I found a safe place to stop. I had just stepped out of the truck, when a man dressed in buckskin pants, no shirt, with beads draped around his neck and a knife sheathed on his belt, sprang in front of the truck. Muscular and fit, his long, dark hair fell in a braid down his back.

He dressed like one might imagine a Native American warrior from eons past.

He angrily demanded to know what I was doing on his land. Since I had lived in the area years before, I knew who owned the adjoining parcels of land and told him that I hadn't realized it was his land.

A raven flew overhead, and he snarled, "See that eagle. It is people like you with your motor vehicles and dogs who are killing the eagles and destroying this land." At that moment, Cuya vaulted from the truck box and ran to my side, a low growl stirring in her throat. The gray hair bristled on the back of her neck. Never had I seen her so agitated. I told her firmly to get back in the truck. Normally, when given a directive, she complied immediately. Cuya was uncanny in her reliability, in this and many other ways. But, on that day, she would not leave my side, even though I repeatedly signaled for her to go back to the truck. By now, the inside of the cab was steaming. The pups were agitated and clamored at the windows, whimpering for fresh air and freedom.

Suddenly, this intruder changed his demeanor radically. His voice became calm, his manner almost seductive. He claimed that he had a camp down through the trees and suggested that I leave the dogs and truck there in the clearing and come to his camp to join him for some tea. At that point, he turned and swaggered down a trail, disappearing into the woods. It is still disturbing when I think of it. Cuya and I turned; an undeniable force swept us back to the truck, through the cover of cedar trees, to the road that would deliver us to safety. We loaded up and straightaway left the area—devastation averted. We drove on, breathing the sweet air, savoring a world that still radiated. Years later, I remember the protective shield that Cuya instinctively created that day. Never had I seen such a reaction from her and wondered if perhaps she was just being especially protective because of her pups.

Tragically, that winter, a teen-aged boy took a walk with his dog into those same woods. At one point he returned home, left his dog, and went back into the woods. The boy's family found this unusual, since he took his dog everywhere with him. Later that evening, when he turned up missing, a search party combed the area, and eventually found his body in a primitive camp in the woods, shot—murdered, and propped against a tree. The rescue party found a note pinned to him, written by the killer that stated he had killed the boy because he had trespassed and was threatening.

A protracted man-hunt ensued that lasted weeks. Eventually, the presumed killer, the man that I had encountered, was captured in another mountain range far away. He was charged with the crime, but chose a defense of insanity. This required that he be brought back to court every six months from the state mental hospital to determine if he could aid in his own defense.

Because my job as a social worker took me to court every week, I saw him when he was brought back to court for these hearings. Over time, whether it was the effects of anti-psychotic drugs or advancing mental illness, this man look ravaged; a wild crazed look stirred in his eyes. I would never have recognized him as the same person. Another state law dictated that a person cannot be held in confinement for more than five years without going to trial. So, at the end of that period, he was released from the state's custody and set free. Case closed.

I still feel deep anguish when I think of that young boy who, innocently, happened into that aboriginal camp and was so callously murdered. What lured him back there without the company and protection of his dog? Perhaps it was the same invitation that I had been offered? Various residents in the area recalled that they had seen this man in the dead of winter, wearing nothing but a loincloth, dancing and chanting. Disconsolate, the community grieved for the boy and his family. And I was immensely grateful for the wisdom and protective instincts that Cuya had demonstrated that day, five years before. She helped us all escape to safety!

Dogs instinctively respond to threats in a natural, watchful manner. Regardless of their size, they use their instincts and heartfelt passions to safeguard and defend the object of their concern. Throughout the centuries, dogs have rescued and comforted the lost and lonely. Saint Bernard of Montjoux, an eleventh century monk during the Augustinian period, founded a monastery high in the Swiss Alps on a road that connected Switzerland and Italy. This road was a common route used by merchants and Swiss workers on their quest for winter employment in Italy, or upon their return home in the summer. People of the northern countries followed this route to make the pilgrimage to Rome. The remote monastery furnished these brave travelers a safe haven from the cold, storms, and alpine hazards.

Saint Bernard and his fellow monks, who had devoted themselves to aiding the lost, wounded or stranded, were aided by large dogs named for Saint Bernard. The monks rarely left the sanctuary without these dogs. Weather conditions could change rapidly, and the mountain fogs made visibility almost impossible. The dogs guided the monks, and those they rescued, back to the shelter of the monastery. These dedicated teams of monks and dogs saved the lives of thousands of travelers.

The most celebrated of the dogs, Barry, rescued forty-four travelers and established a routine that was used by most Saint Bernard rescue dogs. In groups of three, the dogs would set out to search for the lost. And when the rescued traveler was safe, two of the dogs would lie beside him to provide warmth and protection. The third then returned to the monastery to seek help. The dogs themselves made the decision, during each rescue, which two would stay and which one would return. As Stanley Coren describes Saint Bernard:

"It is difficult to dispute the fact that Saint Bernard loved people, having dedicated his life to their rescue. Yet Saint Bernard's affection for dogs ran very deep. Tradition ascribes to him the words 'Qui me amat, amat et canem

meum,' which translates into the familiar expression 'Love me, love my dog.'"[1]

After years of watching dogs display the courage and compassion necessary to accomplish these many missions of mercy, perhaps Saint Bernard, himself, might endorse the belief that the examples of bravery and determination that dogs demonstrate can set a standard for us—a touchstone to use when meeting and conquering our own fears.

As we come to terms with our fears and give them release, joy beckons at the door. We rediscover the roots of our origins; we feel rejuvenated, energized, and confident. Our connection to each other and all other beings—our world—becomes unlimited and bounteous. Joyful experiences are near and far. Possibilities abound in each moment.

Take time to savor the process. Be kind to yourself as you rekindle past delights, and honor the progress you have made—the fears you have mastered, and the freedom you have gained. As you augment your ability to take risks (and a belief in your own personal power), the vision of increased possibilities, your longing for a fuller, more authentic life will expand. No success is small. Each contributes substance and texture to the tapestry of your soul. Allow yourself the luxury of doing less and living more. Be confident that your needs will be met. Have courage, have faith, and then move forward.

Remember your vivid imagination when you played as a child? Participating in the joy of the moment created a juncture to the future, a blank slate with infinite potential. We can still commit to transforming the ordinary into limitless excitement, adventure, expansion, joy and no regrets.

Researcher, Roger Fouts, describes a touching story of Brownie, a dog from his boyhood. Brownie jumped in front of Roger's brother and protected him from an approaching truck, sacrificing her life in the process. Another story which became a media sensation, chronicled another dog who protected a young toddler from deadly snake bites. Even though the dog received many of the snake's bites, he was able to save the young child. Miraculously the dog recovered from the wounds.[2]

During World War I, an Irish soldier who lived in London with his wife and dog, Prince, left home to serve at the front lines. Soon after the soldier departed for the war, Prince disappeared. The soldier's wife searched for Prince, but to no avail. Eventually she wrote her husband the news: that his beloved companion had vanished. She later received a response that, somehow, Prince had located his soldier friend in the war-torn region of northern France. Prince had traveled through London, crossed the English channel, and journeyed over sixty miles, through tear gas and exploding ammunition, to be reunited with his beloved.

America, also, had a canine hero in the same war: Stubby, a homeless bull terrier, was awarded a Victory Medal for his valor, serving with the 102nd Infantry. He was smuggled into France on a troop ship in 1916. He conveyed messages under fire, found wounded soldiers, and stayed with them until their rescuers appeared. Stubby achieved international fame when he woke a dozing sergeant before a planned mustard gas attack occurred, allowing the soldiers enough time to prepare for the assault. He survived 17 battles, including Chateau Thierry, the Marne and the Meuse-Argonne. He was wounded by shrapnel and transferred to a field hospital where his feisty spirit cheered the injured troops.

His service culminated with the soldiers of the 102nd placing a Victory Metal on his collar. Some French women created a cloak for Stubby, and, after each battle, more metals adorned it. After the war, Stubby returned to American a true hero. General Pershing gave him a decoration for "heroism of the highest caliber." The Washington Post proclaimed him the "Sergeant York of animals." He earned lifetime memberships in the American Legion and the Red Cross, participated in parades throughout the country and was greeted by presidents Wilson, Harding and Coolidge for his heroism.

Dogs have protected and comforted American soldiers in every major war effort since that time. Once it was discovered that soldiers were rarely fatalities when accompanied by a dog, 4,000 dogs were sent to accompany our troops during the Vietnam War. Sadly, when the United States forces left Vietnam, the Pentagon declared these dogs to be "war equipment" and ordered that they be "abandoned in place," condemning them to be tortured, eaten or starved to death. How did these dependable, faithful allies respond to this shameful betrayal, this duplicity from those they had protected? We will never know of their fates, the tragedies that befell them, but this is, undoubtedly, a dark, disgraceful chapter in American war history. Surely we can do better.

It is said that fear is the root emotion behind acts of anger. Since dogs tend to deal directly with their fears, their need to express anger is greatly diminished. Like them, each time we face and conquer one of our fears, we are closer to connecting with all things—to the peace and harmony of love, to feeling powerful—emotionally receptive and expressive.

The blissful joy we receive from dogs is poles apart from the satisfaction we receive from our rational endeavors. By receiving their cheer, we experience the prospect of initiating similar social contacts ourselves. Noted Harvard professor, Edward O. Wilson, believes, "To the degree that we come to understand other organisms, we will place greater value on them and on ourselves."[3] He believes that humans have an "inherent need" to be connected with other life forms and the life process, a term he calls "biophilia." This suggests that we are inherently hard-wired to include nature in our daily lives, to be close to animals and plants. Some individuals experience this urging more strongly than others. It is expressed in a desire to share our lives and living spaces with plants and animals regardless of our circumstances. If the need is present and strongly felt, we will find ways to make it happen.[4]

Sofie's lack of fear propelled her into a world of adventure and enchantment. She soared higher and higher and eventually met death on the icy shores of Sourdough Creek. But one look into her eyes, or observing her fervid pursuits, revealed that she eschewed a sheltered, more routine life. And, thus, I watched her soar and one day said, "Good-bye, my little angel, and good journey."

Her every action enhanced her advancement. Her life was as close to perfection, on a consistent basis, as any I have ever witnessed. Sofie embraced her desires and aspired to achieve them—all 14 pounds of her. The Universe bestowed her with the light of courage, a beacon that guided her way. Each day she welcomed adventures she couldn't wait to undertake. She knew what she loved, and had the tenacity to follow her instincts. She created an abundance of love and acceptance in her own life and in those close to her. And, by sharing this benevolence, Sofie helped heal our world.

Does your life seem empty, as if it's missing a vital component? Is there a sense of heaviness that you cannot identify? It could well be that the essential missing element is love. What choices can you make to enrich your life, to pursue your dreams, to stave off regrets? The genesis of these changes comes from within. All we truly have exists in the present moment. It is the whole of what we possess for certain. Ground yourself in the essence of what is truly important to you. The rapture of happiness is easily within reach if we move in that direction with intent.

The time and cause of our death may be unknown to us, but we **can** choose how we will live our remaining days. It *is* possible for us to chart a new course, to take responsibility for being a creator. Develop a willingness to participate fully in each moment—with wisdom, knowledge and purpose.

Be willing to abandon old patterns, old issues, and old thinking. Refuse to be stuck in the quagmire. Do as our dog companions do, say good-bye to the baggage and choose to **live**. Only you can choose your destination. Embrace what is possible in all aspects of your life, and strive to move beyond your comfort level. Each day practice doing things differently—take a new route to work; get up earlier and watch the sunrise; call someone you have wanted to get to know, and invite her or him to lunch. Or, perhaps the best, take a dog on a nature walk, and watch that incredible being in action. Savor every moment, and learn from this master of living. The possibilities are endless.

Dogs are sustained by trust and supported by their emotions and the purity of their intentions. Because of their full engagement in living, dogs transcend their fears, even fear of death. When they do kill, it is almost always for survival or protection. Dogs carry on with confidence that the cycle of life will provide for all their needs—they have no need to domesticate a food supply. Like all animals, if their support system becomes depleted or disappears, dogs unassumingly adapt. And, if that is not possible, they depart into the bosom of the Universal Soul.

In dealing with members of their own species, dominance and submission is established and maintained in ways other than fighting. This cooperative means of communication is essential for numerous reasons, not the least of which is the survival of the species. Nicholas Dodman regards it as "the law of the pack:"[5] the compelling force which establishes a ranking from the alpha (top dog) to the omega (underdog). As long as the hierarchy remains balanced, conflict is minimal, and energy is conserved. However, each tier has the right to the basics, such as food within their possession, and the others, including the alpha, will usually defer. He explains that dogs do not necessarily feel the need to be number one. "They are happy to be second, third or even lower . . . but, it is important for them to know where they stand."[6] This relieves them from the need to feel unnecessarily responsible, and they can proceed with their own interests.

Dogs do what needs to be done—in response to a situation— regardless of the possible repercussions. Sometimes, it appears that they help us even from the spiritual realm.

Scott S. Smith tells the story of two boys rescued by an animal "ghost."

In a town near the Austrian border, twin ten-year-old boys were swimming in the frigid water of Lake Constance. When they both began to flounder, their father swam out to rescue them. Before he could reach them he witnessed the family's collie, Fritz, who had been dead for a year, by their side. Fritz guided them safely to the beach. But as the onlookers rushed to their side, Fritz disappeared. It wasn't just the father who had seen Fritz, but about a dozen eyewitnesses. The police report of this incident confirmed the account.[7]

Each time we face and conquer one of our fears, we solidify our connection with all things, both physical and spiritual—to the peace and harmony of love, to feeling powerful, emotionally receptive and expressive—to all stabilizing forces that are present.

Dogs are patient and fully present in each moment which gives them the confidence to welcome the next moment. They act from their hearts, drawing great strength and courage when the situation demands it. They give endlessly. They are willing to sacrifice everything, even their lives, for those they love. From our association with them, we come to sense what is pure, and moral, and just. We can then embrace it, defend it, and become that goodness.

The more I see of men, the more I admire dogs.
—Jeanne-Marie Roland, French revolutionary (1754-1793)

I can still see my first dog . . . For six years he met me at the same place after school and convoyed me home—a service he thought up himself. A boy doesn't forget that sort of association.
—E. B. White, author (1899-1985)

Chapter 14

TRUST

There was no negative emotion, no doubt, terror or struggle—only complete trust in life and the mystery sustaining life. It was immortality now; eternity palpably present. One wanted to go nowhere, change nothing, just gratefully be. The only urgency was that everyone else should realize the same beatitude, because it belongs to everyone by gift of whatever ineffable mystery is responsible for it. Not that pain and sorrow do not exist. They do, but on a more superficial, impermanent level—perhaps one could say on the training and testing level.[1]

—John Keats

Within the comfort of a loving and trusting environment, we have the opportunity to uncover our creativity. And, as diverse as these processes may be, we discover answers we have been seeking, including our own unique path of peace, harmony and faith. Abiding with and around dogs can help us create such a constructive, nurturing atmosphere. For centuries, people have attested to the remarkable sustenance they have cultivated in their relationships with dogs. We feel unwavering assurance from them and also witness the pure, innocent trust they place in us.

Allen Schoen tells of his extraordinary dog companion and professional mentor, Megan, who came into his life, gravely ill and abandoned, struggling to survive. She was found by a friend of his, begging for food in a parking lot in rural New Hampshire. When she was given food she would devour it and then proceed to cough and collapse on the ground in agony, her eyes pleading for help. From the symptoms described, Shoen was certain that the dog's condition was the potentially fatal heartworm disease. This disorder is caused from tiny worms (microfilaria) that are transmitted from dog to dog through mosquito bites and invade the heart. He told his friend to bring the dog over. At their first meeting he fell in love with Megan. In spite of her profound illness she bounded into his cabin and into his heart as well.

Though Megan was weak and undernourished, Schoen had no choice but to begin the intensive treatments: injections of an arsenic derivative into her bloodstream to prevent the tiny worms from growing to a foot in length and clogging her heart. Schoen believes that Megan knew he was trying to help her, and instead of flinching or trying to avoid the needle, she was completely cooperative, holding up her paw to receive the medication.

Megan's recovery took several months, but eventually she became a vigorous and loving addition to his household and his veterinarian practice. Throughout their years together, Megan became an accomplished healer in her own right. She treated her "patients" with love and compassion, and they *trusted* her presence in their lives.

On one occasion she saved the life of another golden retriever by donating her blood. Megan patiently lifted her paw to meet the needle, just as she had to receive the injections that saved her own life.

Ten years down the road, Megan taught Schoen another important lesson when she developed cancer. At first, she treated herself by regulating her activities. And, just as many humans and animals seek out the benefits of mud packs to reduce inflammation, Megan chose to soak her tumor-ridden body in mud near a natural spring behind his house.

> *Finally, when her time arrived and she could barely move, Megan lay on the floor of our living room, looking up at me as if she knew that we'd never see each other again on this earth. In her eyes I saw the enormous love and gratitude and I hope she saw the same in mine.*

> *When it was time to give her a final injection of euthanasia solution, Megan slowly—and without any prompting—lifted her paw to the needle, the same paw she had raised when I had saved her life and when she'd saved the life of that other retriever. She left this world with the calm grace of a wise soul.[2]*

Every moment is unique and ripe with potential. Each day introduces us to change, both pleasant and challenging, as the cycle of life unfolds. Our animal friends seem able to accept this phenomenon and carry on the best they can.

Unlike some humans, I cannot imagine a dog, who has been well treated, being intentionally cruel or vicious. Attack dogs perform on command to please their human trainers. A dog attacking of its own volition is usually protecting its young or a food source. They may also attack when they feel threatened, or to follow some natural instinct that domesticity has not totally eradicated. Unfortunately, it appears that some dogs who have been overly selectively bred may suffer weaknesses, both physical and mental, that could trigger an unexplained outburst. Since humans are in a position of such control over the lives of many animals, it is imperative that we act responsibly to avert such tragic outcomes.

One light, spring morning, Sofie and I stopped at a yard sale. And, as I followed the sidewalk of an apartment building and rounded the corner, I heard a small bird calling frantically from the rooftop. The bird was in a state of extreme agitation. I glanced behind me and noticed its mate hanging upside down by a long strand of unraveled carpet, dangling helplessly from a second floor deck. It appeared the bird was probably trying to extract the string for nesting material, but somehow the twine became completely wrapped around all of the bird's toes and legs. It was exhausted from struggling and weakened from being inverted—totally incapacitated.

I climbed the stairs and knelt down on the deck. Slowly reeling the bird towards me, I tried to remain calm. What must have been going through its mind? Fortunately, I had a small pair of scissors with me (used for trimming dog hair mats). So, I took out a handkerchief, in which to hold the bird, and slowly and carefully began to clip away the numerous strands, being careful not to injure the small creature.

Throughout the entire procedure, the tiny bird remained very still. I feared that the trauma of the experience would be too much for it to survive. It remained so completely inert that I worried it was in shock, waiting for death. Throughout the rescue process, its mate kept up the animated conversation from the adjoining roof. Was it conveying a warning, fear, or encouragement? Perhaps, it was just willing the stranded one to keep living, to not surrender. I finally came to the last strand, and just as the scissors made their final snip, the immobile bird burst out of my hand and disappeared to join its mate. Its rejuvenation back to life was stunning and exquisite! The pair stopped for a mere second to look at each other, and then Sofie and I watched as they soared off together into the fresh, dew-filled, spring sky.

I was touched by the display of distress and concern from the bird, as it watched its trapped mate, seemingly powerless. But, equally moving was to see them, joined again in flight, relishing the moment with a precise and congenial thoroughness. Perhaps they had envisioned this outcome? They wasted no time in creating the transition, soaring in an altogether creative expression of nature. Ecstatic to resume their adventures, the gates of life opened, affirming their trust, rewarding their forbearance.

Cuya, Little Bear and I shared many such remarkable journeys that joined our souls and strengthened the trust we held for each other. During the time we lived on the farm on the west shore of Flathead Lake, it was our evening ritual to hike up the long, steep hill that sheltered the house. The walk usually lasted around an hour, depending on the route we chose. Eventually we reached the hill top and then settled on a path from a number of possible trails. One that circled back and overlooked the lake, was a favorite. We also had the option of following the mesa, breaking through the tall, native grasses, and discovering the many life-forms that inhabit that flora.

One dusky, summer evening, on one of our walks, Little Bear flushed out a badger. At times he behaved like a hunting dog disguised as an Old English Sheepdog. He was as natural a pointer as any German Shorthair I have seen. Anyone who has ever encountered one of these formidable creatures knows instantly that the prudent course is to give the badger a wide birth and not provoke an attack. Little Bear was only about two at the time and still vulnerable to puppy curiosity and impulsivity.

He and the badger stared at each other, nose to nose, for what seemed an eternity. There was an air of electricity between them. Little Bear was, by far, much larger, but the badger's dental display showed firm evidence that it did not feel threatened in the least. Slowly and gracefully, Little Bear ultimately deferred. Backing away, and with a prolonged gesture, he lowered his eyes, conveying respect, and offered his version of a truce. Gratefully, I gathered the two dogs, and on we proceeded. No vet bills that night!

On another of our treks, we crossed the ridge top, intrigued by a large herd of pack horses and mules that had been put out to pasture over the winter. It had been months since they had seen a human, and, perhaps even longer since they had encountered a canine. Since I was raised on a ranch, I had a strong affinity for horses. Cuya had grown up around the two saddle horses that I boarded and rode on the south shore, so the chance to contact the equine world appealed to us both. As we approached the herd in the vast pasture, it soon became apparent that our presence was not welcomed. The herd began to circle us, closing in, their ears laid back, teeth bared, snorting and stamping. Cuya just wanted to make friends, and Little Bear was at a total loss as to what to make of all of this. Since there were twenty to thirty of these massive beasts, I knew that our status in the hierarchy was grim.

Fortunately, I had tied a jacket around my waist before we left home, in case we were caught in the chill of the evening. I waved the jacket over my head and around us, and bellowed at the pack string in as stern a tone as I could muster—trying to establish some air of authority. Maneuvering our group, with a death grip on Little Bear's collar, and constantly directing Cuya to stay beside me, we slowly inched our way across the field. Hoping for more life beyond that hour, I knew that if somehow we could pass through the danger, at the end, we might somehow have a laugh.

We learned a valuable lesson that day. I had never witnessed horses displaying such aggression, but it was clear that they considered us encroachers. I believe that, given half a chance, they would have stomped and bit us to death. Through some benevolent force of grace, they showed respect for a waving jacket and my fierce, forceful posture. The dogs and I were grateful that we had each other that day and chalked up another of life's lessons to faith and fortitude and *trust* in each other.

Essential to our advancement is the ability to let go of any expected outcome, trusting that the correct solution will present itself. Having this faith proceeds from having a loving, trusting nature and, in this arena, dogs, and perhaps all animals, are supreme practitioners.

Dogs can nurture and guide us through phases of our lives. They assist our growth with loving regard, and we can do the same for them. And when we are both ready for the next stage, they depart from our lives, knowing we can go on, expanded and enriched. Dogs are not equipped with high technology or lethal weapons. They face life supplied with conviction and love. They have the possession of their life-force, the courage to keep trying. They are blessed with trust and it carries them far. What a miraculous trait.

For months after Cuya had passed on to the spirit world, I reflected back on the many remarkable adventures we shared and the uncommon bond of trust we had forged with each other. It seemed as though I could not pay her a high enough tribute, but I made an attempt in this letter to my rare and loyal friend:

October 27, 1991
My Dearest friend Cuya,

I had to say "Good-bye" to you yesterday, dear friend, but, it really wasn't good-bye—for I will hold you in my heart forever. You brought such joy and happiness to my life; your goodness and loving spirit will be with me always. You were so beautiful in every way and I thank you for sharing the same path with me for so long.

Today it snowed eight inches, and I feel at peace that you no longer have to struggle against it. In recent years, the snow and cold were hard for you, aggravating your arthritis. But, I remember when you came into my life, how much you loved the snow! As a puppy, you rode on the ends of my cross country skis because the snow was so deep that year. I have some lovely pictures of you and Scruff in our ski paths. You two were so magnificent! Hearty, robust—what a splendid winter we had that year!

This weekend, I told many important people about your passing. They were so kind in their comments. They knew how vital you were to my life and how much I will miss you. I hope you are happy . . . free and light. I felt your presence today as I walked and trust you are in a kindly place, perhaps with Scruff, your beloved father.

You were so divine—my dream puppy. Two black ears, beautiful dark eyes—your physical beauty was matched by your loving spirit, an archetype feminine personality, maternal, nurturing, instinctive and loving.

But, you were also active: running with your puppies, jumping on top of your dog house, climbing your favorite tree beside the river in Polson. We saved each other's lives at least once that I recall. You, by dispersing that feral dog pack south of town, pinning the lead Doberman in a flash. And, I, when Little Bear was so young, skirting that herd of menacing wild pack horses and mules, with both of you close by my side—waving my jacket and yelling, for what seemed an eternity, until they lost interest in their attack.

One of my favorite memories is of you and your puppies in the spring of 1980. Scruff was no longer with us, God bless him, and you were only three years old. You were such a conscientious mother. We had so much fun romping in the park with the puppies! People who had been watching the raising of the Retta Mary, after it sank in the bay, drove by slowly—to stare at your incredible family. The pups grew up quickly, and they were soon gone to other homes. We kept Little Bear, and what a splendid friend and companion he was to us both.

You two stayed alone on the farm for six weeks, with Jan checking in and feeding you when I went to Europe. You seemed so happy on that Flathead grange. For so much of your life, you were able to run freely in nature—to have the kind of life that an Old English Sheepdog relishes. Over the years many people remarked about the beauty of your spirit, and asked about you. In truth, they were genuinely interested. You touched the lives of so many in a deep and meaningful way.

Pictures from the early days show your lovable qualities—what an angel! Beautiful knowing eyes, strong energy, always a vital part of the action. And, such a stunning coat. Sturdiness—a creature containing a thousand hugs and willing to share them with many so fortunate recipients. You were extraordinary, like your father, from the very beginning. Some people questioned why I wanted or needed two Old English Sheepdogs, but I knew you were both significant to my life.

Scruff became ill when you were still a puppy and died when you were barely one. The grief I felt seemed unbearable—I could find no consolation. But, you were always there, by my side, and we developed a beautiful relationship. I was so pleased and proud to share my life with you. You spread joy and amazement wherever you went, loving everyone, especially children.

You and Little Bear remained a remarkable duo for five years. I was comforted, knowing you had each other, since I was gone so much then. But, when we moved to Bozeman, Little Bear could not to cope with the stimulation of city life. He felt threatened and became overly-protective. The day we said good-bye to him up was another period of extreme grief for me. He was such a beauty—so strong, athletic and smart—a natural pointer. Remember our walk when he flushed out the badger? It broke my heart to see him leave to live on the farm at Ennis, and I heard that he mourned us greatly as well. Even though he was not fond of men, his new family had two teen-aged boys who adored him. They did all they could to comfort him. Perhaps learning to trust men was a lesson he was meant to learn. We all made tremendous sacrifices to move to Bozeman, but, through it all, you were there with me.

My dearest Cuya, you were so tolerant of my life— such a kind and gentle support to me— whatever my mood. I gave my best effort to care for you and give you what you needed. But, if I let you down in any way, I apologize. My love and concern for you is unwavering and eternal.

And now grief is re-visiting, but greatly amplified. Taking you to the vet for euthanasia was the hardest thing I have ever done. If there would have been any other way, I would have chosen it. But, dear one, your life seemed to contain little joy anymore. Physically, you must have been in pain, and you seemed confused because your sight and hearing were almost gone. I made the decision out of love and respect for you, to allow you to die with dignity and comfort, surrounded by love. To free your beautiful spirit to soar wherever you please. But, in my heart, I wanted to keep you here with me forever.

My dear, loving friend, may you always be happy and free. You deserve only the best. Letting you go was painful beyond words. I hope you understand. Every moment I miss your presence. Each time I do something for the first time without you, I feel the void and the throb in my heart. I know you are no longer suffering, and I pray you are in a better place. But, the loss feels far too great right now.

That first day, I wondered how you were adjusting to the spirit world. You had such a determined spirit for life. My friend, you were so strong, and through every adversity, fought to stay in the physical world. It must have been so difficult to let that go.

I sent you on ahead, to the great Creator, with abounding love—not wanting it happen, yet recognizing that we all must cross that threshold at some point. If the quality of our lives contributes to our evolution, you surely made great strides from this lifetime. Even though your life span was shorter, in years, than mine, we shared our very best years together. Two vibrant female spirits, in the glory of our prime! Alas, my decline will take longer, and so, it was necessary that we part ways, for now, on our great journey through the cosmos.

I know not what follows, yet I have a strong sense that the Life Force continues in some form. And, I cannot imagine that a connection as strong as ours would ever be severed. I yearn to join you someday, reunited in the spirit world. I know, as the distractions of this world have their effects, it may appear that my attention lessens. But, this is only temporary and not nearly important as it may seem. Nothing is more important than love—it is eternal. We may not always give it top priority, but, if we had good sense, as you did, we would. I will always love you and remember your warmth and devotion. Nothing that will happen in the future will ever displace that. You are gloriously unique, like Scruff and Little Bear and Mister. I will cherish you all forever, and be eternally grateful for all that we shared in this life.

For the past twenty years I have had the solid, support of Old English Sheepdog love. It is hard to imagine life without it. Oh, this physical life, Cuya! It comes with its lessons and trials and grief, as one life-form changes into another. But, love transcends all. Thank you for joining my life and extending such high esteem and regard. That will be our bond throughout eternity. You are my treasure. I will love you forever. It is hard to go on without you, so difficult to say good-bye.

No one can ever take your place. You taught me so much about love; maybe now, I can be more open to human love. I think I can do that now. You made me feel safe enough to open my heart to love. I pay you the highest tribute as loyal and loving friend. I am very fortunate to have known your faithfulness and shared your path, a creature of such noble integrity. Thank you, from the depths of my soul.

Forever your devoted friend, Dorothy

In keeping with the vivid examples of animals risking their lives and well-being for humans, there are times when it behooves us to take risks on our own behalf. If we are open to it, animals can bring us the threefold gifts of risk, adventure and discovery. With their guidance, we can come to celebrate changes in place, attitude, and circumstance. We can learn to welcome rather than fear change. We can also come to relish risk instead of studiously avoiding it.[3]

—Susan Chernak McElroy

What makes dogs want to be near us, to touch their bodies to ours? There is something wonderful about my dog's stretching her body along my body at night, something about the trust it shows. That is one of the most touching things about being in a deep relationship with a member of another species: the mutual trust. "I know," the dog seems to be saying, "that nothing bad will happen to me if I'm with you. I can relax my whole body and trust that you will not harm me while I sleep."[4]

—Jeffrey Masson

Chapter 15

HEALING

*Healing is the growth that each person seeks. Healing is
what happens when we come to our edge, to the unexplored
territory of mind and body, and take a single step beyond into
the unknown, the space in which all growth occurs. Healing
is discovery. It goes beyond life and death. Healing occurs
not in the tiny thoughts of who we think we are and what we
know, but in the vast undefinable spaciousness of being—of
what we essentially are . . .[1]*

—Stephen Levine

*One reason a dog can be such a comfort when you're feeling
blue is that he doesn't try to find out why.*

—Author unknown

As I wrote this book on the banks of Sourdough Creek, trying
to gain some understanding of Sofie's death, I encountered varying
forms of the winter and spring weather patterns of the northern
Rockies. Some days the midday sun warmed the grass and rocks with
the promise of new life. Other days, menacing blizzard winds assailed
me with icy pellets. The frigid temperatures numbed my fingers, fur-
ther accentuating the absence of Sofie's warm, loving companionship.
As snow settled on my writing pads, the moisture rippled the paper,

creating lasting, unmistakable evidence of this unrelenting interval of reflection, of change, and, ultimately, the creation of an altered form.

The mere presence of dogs can generate extraordinary healing effects on those who are suffering physically or emotionally. The dominant life emotions that dogs emit towards humans is a combination of love, loyalty and closeness which helps arouse the emotions of our hearts and heal the empty spaces. With this devotion and life-enriching strength bestowed on us, it becomes possible for us to accept this safe space for release and rejuvenation.

Green Chimneys Children Services at Brewster, NY, combines a five acre farm and wildlife conservation center with therapy services for adolescent children who are emotionally disturbed, or at risk to commit violent behavior. The facility is a sanctuary for animals who have been rescued from abusive situations. They are able to live out their lives there, in a protected, secure environment.

The residents are actively involved in the care of the animals, and the effects of these relationships have produced success beyond measure for both the children and animals. Both sides have learned, over time, that they can trust another being and that trust will bring goodness to their lives. When rescue workers bring animals to the center, they sometimes arrive in an ambulance—the officers wearing full uniforms. The youths see, ". . . that there are officials out there who care about animals, and that there's no reason to fear law enforcement."[2]

The founder of FLY-N-K9, certified handler, Johnny McGuire, trains therapy animals to assist patients with physical ailments. He trained his therapy partner, an Australian shepherd named Baby, who was born deaf, to recognize almost 70 hand signals. She is involved in the treatment plans of many of the residents of the Ten Broeck Commons Nursing and Rehabilitation Center in Lake Katrine, NY. McQuire tells of Baby's "sense about people. She will always approach the neediest person in the room and in her own way figure out what's special about that person." McQuire encourages others, who have an interest in becoming involved in animal therapy to "get your animal evaluated, and then, listen and learn."[3]

Jewel, a standard poodle who is associated with the Manhattan-based ASPCA/Delta Pet Partners, and her partner, Karen Le Frak, work with patients who have spinal cord trauma and head injuries at Mount Sinai. One day, a young male patient wanted to see Jewel, but because of concern for asthmatic patients, hospital administrators were hesitant to allow Jewel into the hospital. The dilemma was solved when the Pet Partner team walked up eight flights of stairs and met the boy on the rooftop. Le Frak remembers the meeting, "His face lit up like a Christmas tree when he saw Jewel. He walked her with his IV tubes coming out of one hand and the leash in the other."[4]

Can our healing be enhanced just by knowing that we are in the presence of a being so noble, honest, and loving? Or, do these powerful healers inspire us to find these very qualities within ourselves, thus elevating our own development and advancement—so that our own true enlightenment can occur? Perhaps it is possible for us to receive this protective closeness from dogs when we may not feel an open trust to accept it in other forms.

Research from the University of Nebraska School of Medicine of several hundred elderly people showed that those who were involved in a close relationship possessed better immune function and lower cholesterol levels. Over the past few years, other substantial investigations have reached a similar conclusion: close relationships do promote good health.[5] But, for some individuals, although the *possibility* for intimacy may be all around them, many find it lacking in their own lives. Romance may elude them; family members may be distant; or the confidence to succeed in a connected relationship may be compromised. Social isolation can occur for many reasons.

Dogs, as companions, can provide a bond, a connection to solving this detrimental condition. Because they give so openly and unselfishly, dogs help us to overcome these social barriers. They remind us to strive for our best, to believe in our best (which is the state of love). They give us that love; they give us a better life.

We have witnessed that dogs with disabilities don't wallow in self pity. They immediately set about making the necessary adaptations to get on with life—continuing to generate love with a passion and zest for life, despite the major adjustment. They demonstrate the value of perseverance to overcome obstacles, including physical challenges. These brave creatures show us the value and meaning of embracing each moment, even routine, everyday occurrences. They appreciate that each moment is precious and holds the possibility to learn, to love, and to evolve. They make the most of the time they have.

The more we capture the benevolence available to us in the Universe, the better able we are to weather the ups and downs that are a part of life. Susan Chernak McElroy tells the story of Chelsea, a courageous Labrador who lost her eyesight from diabetes. Her caregiver, Patty Aguirre, who is a physical therapist, was urged by her friends to do the humane thing and have Chelsea euthanized. Patty, herself, wondered if she was being selfish by refusing euthanasia until Chelsea would wag her tail with all the enthusiasm for life of a sighted dog. So, Patty set about training Chelsea to meet the challenges presented by her blindness. She found balls that made noise and sugar-free treats to give Chelsea as a reward after her painful insulin injections. She taught her the commands, "Up" and "Down," as a warning for stairs. Chelsea now knows, "Watch out!" as a warning of an object in her path. They also warn her with "shot" so she is not frightened when given her injections. Patty shares the inspiration Chelsea has brought to her life:

> Chelsea brings out the best is all of us. She teaches us to look for the value of life; she helps us look past the physical problems. She is a living example of perseverance. Through her, I have learned new tools to use in my quest to reach people who have given up. Each time she returns from the lake tri-

umphant, dripping wet with a stick in her mouth, I look deep into vacant eyes and see her lion's heart.[6]

For those of us who have been traumatized, our canine allies offer a safe and loving arena in which to face our fears. Dogs seem to know instinctively when we are in pain. Through their licks, tail-wagging, and desire to be close, they help us to feel better about ourselves and the world around us. Since dogs have maintained their attunement with the natural world, they can inspire us to pay more attention to our own senses and innate abilities. Their exceptional ability to remain in the present can calm us—help ground us in reality. The more often we enter this state, the more contentment we experience. Dogs don't need success, money or accolades to find peace, and once we have achieved this state of personal security, neither should we. As we observe dogs and how they approach the life experience, they appear to be as much "of the soul" as they are "of the body."

It is essential for dogs and other actualizing personalities to be aware of their emotions and allow them expression. To stifle this process creates neurosis, depression and maladaptive behaviors. By keeping ourselves separate, we grow anxious—our potential and self-esteem thwarted. If, instead, we choose to love, share and interact, we grow, and thus, begin to actualize our *Wholeness*. When we release fear and choose to trust, we open ourselves to the wonder and support of endless comforting systems. And that foundation can shepherd within us the confidence to reveal our unique gifts to the world.

The lure to our self-absorbed, underdeveloped identities, is the shallow, fleeting and illusionary gains of money, fame, or other materialistic gains. But, when we attain release, the reward, even at the eventual price of death, is grace and the knowledge that we have advanced our souls and made an eternal contribution to the healing of the planet.

Dogs direct their energies to the common good by caring about and healing others in their amiable ways. This can be confirmed by the love that is conveyed in their eyes. They give us their undivided attention and are present with us in a humble, gentle manner. The compassionate dog-lover, Laura, in the book *Beautiful Joe*, believed that, if there were ever a species worthy of entrance into heaven, it was the dog. As she tells the story: "Well, when Adam was turned out of paradise, all the animals shunned him, and he sat weeping bitterly with his head between his hands, when he felt the soft tongue of some creature gently touching him. He took his hands from his face, and there was a dog who had separated himself from all the other animals and was trying to comfort him. He became the chosen friend and companion of Adam, and afterward of all men."[7]

When Sofie and I would drive down the road, she routinely sat in my lap, hoping I would crack the window and let her join the world of scents splitting the breezes. Her wee black nose bobbed in the currents, following invisible fissures of aromas, hoping for a wilder ride. She would gaze up into my face, for long periods of time, with the most adoring look—as if she were committing everything about me to her memory. Perhaps she was doing her own assessment of me, trying to determine my mood, or read what she thought I needed. She placed her head in my lap; I placed my hand on her head. That was the answer. Months after her death, remembering the poignancy of these moments made me even more grateful for every hug we shared, every pat on the head, and every kind word I ever spoke to her. My memories of her remarkable presence in my life helped me heal from the dreadful, aching void I felt after her passing. As John Welsons reminds us:

> *The healing of grief begins when we allow our hearts to be open and vulnerable, when we allow ourselves into them, and allow our wounds and sorrows to be healed by them. While our cultural conditioning has been to close our hearts at times of sadness or fear, the true healing takes place when we open them to absorb our darkness, and swallow it into the infinite light they contain.*[8]

For many years, dogs have been successfully trained to provide service and therapy. The most well-known are the trained guide dogs that assist the visually impaired. But, in recent years, therapy dogs meet a wide range of needs for individuals by providing support, motivation and the comfort of their presence. Service animals are also trained to perform specific tasks unique to the needs of a disabled person.

We all have traumas to overcome in our lives. These experiences teach us valuable lessons. At the very least, we glean examples of what we do *not* want to do, or become—highlighting areas of our souls that need assistance. We must discover new images for ourselves and change our beliefs accordingly. If we are to achieve our higher visions, we must receive these lessons as gifts and use them to gain a broader perspective of what is possible. As we integrate what we **believe** with what we **desire**, our soul is expanded, and we draw nearer to our Higher Self.

Dogs show us how to live from the heart, which helps us on our journey towards wholeness. This enhances the emotional healing that occurs from this exchange and transforms our lives. Dogs serve as examples of how to conduct ourselves in loving relation to each other and in union with another higher, nobler reality. This reality heals our emotional wounds, allowing us to start anew with our hearts opened and cleared. Dogs can achieve this from the simple act of making us feel comfortable.

A humorous account tells the tale of a famous man seeking the comfort that dogs bestow. The author Edmund Fuller wrote: "Thomas A. Edison was once reluctantly persuaded by his wife to attend one of the big social functions of the season in New York. At last the inventor managed to escape the crowd of people vying for his attention, and sat alone in a corner. Edison kept looking at his watch with a resigned expression on his face. A friend edged near to him unnoticed and heard the inventor mutter to himself with a sigh, 'If there were only a dog here!'"

By touching this inner need for love and acceptance, we begin the healing process that fosters emotional security. We activate our experience of the divine sense of order, and our resistance and fears fall away. Because of the gentle and patient kindnesses that dogs visit upon us, we, too, can learn the value of mercy. In the mystic tradition, dogs maintain awareness in their encounters. They respond spontaneously to others in need and can help us achieve a state of wholeness—a state only fully attained in conjunction with a spiritual quest. Their consistently loving actions demonstrate a truly enlightened state of consciousness, and, if that is our course, they can expedite our journey.

If we are open, dogs can be our kind and loving teachers. They will gently guide and support us through the many phases of our lives and enhance our personal self confidence—our ability to feel and express emotions. Going for a walk with a dog is an example. Activity seems to enhance our natural inclination to explore this area of our lives; increasing physical movement augments our capacity to relax our bodies. As we explore the environment that surrounds us, our minds are calmed, allowing feelings and creative inspirations from our highest level an open door for expression.

By overcoming our fears, we take a first major step towards rebirth. We risk losing the common and familiar aspects of our lives in the process, but gain a new life as a result. The fears that gripped us and stilted our lives, no longer paralyze our forward progress. As we open our hearts, the love that is released makes all things new again. Even though everything is constantly changing, we still lose nothing. In truth, in this expanded state, our soul, our essence, our very *beings* are strengthened, affirmed, and made greater as our growth and evolution continue.

Our spiritual growth and emotional health is as vitally important as anything else we may achieve in our lives. I had encountered the opportunities to *share love* many times before, but not always with great success. Sofie and Cuya helped me resurrect that part of my self that was urgently in need of renewal. They validated my belief that it was safe to love, to be open, to be vulnerable. As my confidence grew, and I became more receptive, it generated within me, the energy to express my creative urgings. My character was strengthened as I began to realize more of my inspired desires, to feel more secure about myself and my life.

Dogs' selfless service to humans solidifies their inestimable value, a worth of high and noble honor. We can nurture and bless their spiritual exemplifications to give and serve by following their example, by honoring all of life in the highest manner possible. Dogs give us emotional support, inspiration to express our emotions, and a feeling of safety as we cast loose the chains that bind our hearts. We, in turn, gain the courage and trust to reciprocate this regard towards them and others in our lives. As this love is released, not only are we healed, our animal healers are advanced, and the entire planet benefits from the increased state of peace, harmony and developing trust.

> *The psychological and moral comfort of a presence at once humble and understanding—this is the greatest benefit that the dog has bestowed upon man.*
> —Percy Blysshe Shelley, British poet (1792-1822)

> *His ears were often the first thing to catch my tears.*
> [Speaking about her cocker spaniel, Flush]
> —Elizabeth Barrett Browning, English poet (1806-1861)

> *A faithful friend is a strong protection.*
> *A person who has found one has found a treasure.*
> *A faithful friend is beyond price,*
> *And his value cannot be weighed.*
> *A faithful friend is a life-giving medicine.*
> —The Apocrypha

Chapter 16

A Love Tribute to Dogs

A life lived in the service of humanity, a love of and respect for all living things—those attributes are the essence of saint-like behavior.

—Jane Goodall

I know well enough that there have been dogs so loving that they have thrown themselves into the same grave with the dead bodies of their masters; others have stayed upon their masters' graves without stirring a moment from them, and have voluntarily starved themselves to death, refusing to touch the food that was brought to them.

—Miguel de Cervantes, Spanish author (1547-1616)

I think God will have prepared everything for our perfect happiness [in Heaven]. If it takes my dog being there, I believe he'll be there.

—Rev. Billy Graham, evangelist (b. 1918)

It is true that whenever a person loves a dog he derives great power from it.

—Old Seneca chief

Dog! When we first met on the highway of life, we came from the two poles of creation . . . What can be the meaning of the obscure love for me that has sprung up in your heart?
—Anatole France, French author (1844-1924)

I love my dear mistress; I can say more than that; I love her better than anyone else in the world.
—Margaret Marshall Saunders, from *Beautiful Joe*

Dogs love company. They place it first in their short list of needs.
—J. R, Ackerley

The dog has an enviable mind. It remembers the nice things in life and quickly blots out the nasty.
—Barbara Woodhouse

It is a strange thing, love. Nothing but love has made the dog lose his wild freedom, to become the servant of man.
—D. H. Lawrence

Not Carnegie, Vanderbilt, and Astor together could have raised money enough to buy a quarter share in my little dogs.
—Ernest Thompson Seton

He cannot be a gentleman which loveth not a dog.
—John Northbrooke

If you think you have influence, try ordering someone else's dog around.
—Anonymous

The one absolutely unselfish friend that a man can have in this selfish world, the one that never deserts him . . . is his dog. A man's dog stands by him in prosperity and poverty, in health and sickness. He will sleep on the cold ground, when the wintry winds blow and the snow drives fiercely, if only he can be near his master's side. He will kiss the hand that has no food. He guards the sleep of a pauper as if he were a prince. If fortune drives the master forth, an outcast in the world, the faithful dog asks no higher privilege than that of accompanying him to guard against danger, to fight against his enemies, and when the last scene of all comes, and death takes the master in its embrace, there by his grave side will the noble dog be found, his head between his paws, his eyes sad but open in alert watchfulness, faithful and true.

—George Graham Vest

If the history of all the dogs who have loved and been loved by the race of man could be written, each history of a dog would resemble all the other histories. It would be a love story.

—James Douglas

As I reflect on the times shared with the mystical dog partners who have guided my path, the manner that they entered and departed this world, and the lessons we learned, I feel infinitely grateful for their company, for the comfort and the joys they brought, and continue to impart to my life each day.

By respecting the range of our canine companions, watching them move in the rhythm of their lives; we catch a glimpse of another order, a sage and natural cadence. They seem to achieve solace by measuring it everywhere. This comfort may be their antidote to life, where power and control often come up short. Dogs accommodate the changes of life with an exquisite blend of strength and fragility. Natural mediators, their genuine characters defy false appearance in the inscrutable, laconic world they often encounter. They inspire a belief that emotional evolution is possible. Passion, intuition and tenderness can indeed conquer logic, the rumble of lethargy, the redundancies of death and creation. Dogs hold us in the present.

How wise are dogs to make loyalty and forgiveness, joy and devotion their priorities. Let us learn from them. May we find the space in our hearts to honor their hallowed, courageous, tolerant souls. May we begin a quest and disappear into a confluence of who we might become. And, may we be inspired by our dog companions to develop and expand our own characters, our personas, and our integrity—to emulate their life-giving ability to give and receive love.

BIBLIOGRAPHY

Anderson, Allen, and Linda. *Angel Animals*. New York: Penguin Putnam.

Bass, Rick. *Colter*. New York: Houghton Mifflin Company, 2000.

Burnham, Sophy. *The Ecstatic Journey*. New York: Ballatine Books, 1997.

Caras, Roger. *A Dog Is Listening*. New York: Simon & Schuster, 1992.

Carson, David, and Sams, Jamie. *Medicine Cards*. Santa Fe, NM: Bear & Company, 1988.

Cohen, J. M., and Phipps, J. F. *Common Experience*. Wheaton, IL: Quest Books, 1992.

Coren, Stanley. *Why We Love the Dogs We Do*. New York: Simon & Schuster, 1998.

Cramer, Ben. "They Were Heroes Too", *Parade Magazine*, (April 1, 2001), p.4.

Cutler, Howard, C. and His Holiness The Dalai Lama. *The Art Of Happiness*. New York: Penguin Putnam, Inc., 1998

Dodman, Nicholas, H. *The Dog Who Loved Too Much*. New York: Bantam Books, 1996.

DuBay, Connie, ed. *Speak!* New York: Penguin Putnam Inc., 2000.
Fox, Matthew. Creation Spirituality. New York: Harper Collins Publishers, 1991

Fox, Matthew, and Sheldrake, Rupert. *Natural Grace*. New York: Doubleday Dell Publishing Group, 1997.

Garber, Marjorie. *Dog Love*. New York: Simon & Schuster, 1996.

Goodall, Jane. *Reason for Hope*. New York: Warner Books, 1999.

"Healing Partnerships", *ASPCA Animal Watch* (Spring, 2001), p.29.

Herriot, James. *Dog Stories*. New York: St. Martin's Press, 1972.

Hunt, Laurel, ed. *Angel Pawprints*. New York: Hyperion, 1998.

Kowalski, Gary, A. *Goodbye, Friend*. Walpole, NH: Stillpoint Publishing, 1997.

_________________. *The Souls of Animals*. Walpole, NH: Stillpoint Publishing, 1999

Kundera, Milan. *The Unbearable Lightness of Being*. New York: Harper & Row Publishers, 1984.

Masson, Jeffrey Moussaieff. *Dogs Never Lie About Love*. New York: Three Rivers Press, 1997

McElroy, Susan Chernak. *Animals as Guides for the Souls*. New York: Ballatine Publishing Group, 1998

_________________. *Animals as Teachers and Healers*. New York: Ballatine Publishing Group, 1997.

Morris, Willie. *My Dog Skip*. New York: Random House, 1995.

Randour, Mary Lou. *Animal Grace*. Novato, CA: New World Library, 2000.

Saunders, Marshall. *Beautiful Joe*. Bedford, MA: Applewood Books, 1894.

Schaffer, Dylan. *Dog Stories*. San Francisco: Chronicle Books, 1997.

Schoen, Allen, J. *Kindred Spirits*. New York: Random House, 2001.

Sinetar, Marsha. *Ordinary People as Monks and Mystics*. New York: Paulist Press, 1986

Steinbeck, John. *Travels with Charley*. New York: Viking Press, 1961.

Stanley, Gary. *What My Dog Has Taught Me About Life*. Tulsa, OK: Honor Books, 1999.

Teasdale, Wayne. *Mystic Heart*. Novato, CA: New World Library, 1999.

Underhill, Evelyn. *Mysticism*. Oxford: Oneworld Publications, 1993.

Welshons, John, E. *Awakening from Grief*. Little Falls, NJ: Open Heart Publications, 2000

NOTES AND REFERENCES

Chapter One
1. Underhill, *Mysticism*, pp. 86-87.
2. Quoted in Cohen and Phipps, *The Common Experience*, p. 175.
3. Underhill, *Mysticism*, p. 71.
4. S. P. Swami and W. B. Yeats, *The Ten Principal Upanishads*.
5. Burnham, *The Ecstatic Journey*, p. 3.
6. Ibid., p. 4.

Chapter Two
1. Bass, *Colter*, p. 85.

Chapter Three
1. Wigton, personal correspondence.

Chapter Four
1. Morris, *My Dog Skip*, p. 1.
2. Law, *Selected Mystical Writings of William Law*.
3. Randour, *Animal Grace*, p. 27.
4. Schoen, *Kindred Spirits*, p. 176.
5. Kundera, *The Unbearable Lightness of Being*, pp. 297-298.
6. Masson, *Dogs Never Lie About Love*, p.31.

Chapter Five
1. Herriot, *Dog Stories*, p. xii.
2. Kowalski, *The Souls of Animals*, p. 18.
3. Burnham, *The Ecstatic Journey*, pp. 96-97.
4. Fox and Sheldrake, *Natural Grace*, p. 63.
5. Cohen and Phipps, *The Common Experience*, p. 83.

6. Scott and Fuller, *Genetics and the Social Behavior of the Dog*, p. 137.

7. Randour, *Animal Grace*, p. 17.

8. Masson, *Dogs Never Lie About Love*, p. 44.

9. McElroy, *Animals as Teachers and Healers*, p. 18.

10. Taschen, *A Thousand Hounds*, p. 238.

11. Kundera, *The Unbearable Lightness of Being*, pp. 131-132.

12. Caras, *A Dog is Listening*, pp. 138-139.

Chapter Six

1. Fox and Sheldrake, *Natural Grace*, p. 117.

2. McElroy, *Animals as Guides for the Soul*, p. 7.

3. Burnham, *The Ecstatic Journey*, p. 19.

4. Underhill, *Mysticism*, p. 24.

5. Krishnamurti, *The Second Penguin Krishnamurti Reader*.

6. Quoted in Fox and Sheldrake, *Natural Grace*, p. 88.

7. Quoted in Cohen and Taylor, *Dogs and Their Women*, p. 52.

8. Trungpa, *Meditation in Action*.

9. Quoted in Sinetar, *Ordinary People as Monk and Mystics*, p. 148.

10. Bass, *Colter*, p. 171.

11. Cohen and Phipps, *The Common Experience*, pp. 28, 31-32.

12. Masson, *Dogs Never Lie About Love*, p. 36.

13. Weber and Schaffer, *Dog Stories*, p. 16.

14. Fox and Sheldrake, *Natural Grace*, p. 34.

Chapter Seven

1. Burnham, *The Ecstatic Journey*, p. 183.

2. Quoted in Cohen and Phipps, *The Common Experience*, p. 84.

3. Evans-Wentz, *Tibet's Great Yogi, Milarepa*.

4. His Holiness The Dalai Lama and Cutler, *The Art of Happiness*, pp. 116-117.

5. Trumler, *Understanding Your Dog*.

6. Kundera, *The Unbearable Lightness of Being*, p. 289.

7. Thurber, *The Fireside Book of Dog Stories*, p. xiii of the Introduction.

8. His Holiness the Dalai Lama and Cutler, *The Art of Happiness*, p. 56.

9. Halifax, *A Buddhist Life in America*, p. 2.

10. Picher, *The Dogs Who Came to Stay*, p. 66.

11. Hyland, *The Slaughter of Terrified Beasts: A Biblical Basis for the Humane Treatment of Animals*, p. 1.

12. Fox, *Creation Spirituality*, p.97.

Chapter Eight

1. Maeterlinck, *Our Friend the Dog*, pp. 62-63.

2. Garber, *Dog Love*, p. 244.

3. Schoen, *Kindred Spirits*, p. 194.
4. Herriot, *Dog Stories*, p. 72.
5. Ibid., p. 73.
6. Ibid., pp. 74-77.
7. Regan, "The Bird in the Cage: A Glimpse of My Life," *Between the Species*, vol. 2 (1986): pp. 42-49 and 90-100.
8. Randour, *Animal Grace*, pp. 35-36.
9. Fox and Sheldrake, *Natural Grace*, pp. 69-70.
10. Masson, *Dogs Never Lie About Love*, p. 24.
11. Ibid., pp. 24-25.
12. Underhill, *Mysticism*, p. 18.
13. Fox, *Creation Spirituality*, pp. 86-87.

Chapter Nine
1. Steinbeck, *Travels with Charley*, pp. 13-14.
2. Ibid., p. 238.
3. His Holiness the Dalai Lama and Cutler, *The Art of Happiness*, p. 249.
4. Stanley, *What My Dog Has Taught Me About Life*, p. 180.
5. Ibid., pp. 181-182.
6. Morris, *My Dog Skip*, p. 120.

Chapter Ten
1. McElroy, *Animals As Guides For The Soul*, p. 11.
2. Sams and Carson, *Medicine Cards*, pp. 69-70.
3. Morris, *My Dog Skip*, pp. 121-122.
4. Weber and Schaffer, *Dog Stories*, p. 30.
5. McElroy, *Animals As Guides For The Soul*, p. 190.
6. Kundera, *The Unbearable Lightness of Being*, p. 292.
7. Quoted in Winokur, ed., *Mondo Canine*, p. 234.
8. Kowalski, *Good-bye Friend*, p. 67.
9. Bass, *Colter*, pp. 176-177.
10. Ibid., p. 170.
11. Garber, *Dog Love*, pp. 282-282.
12. Ibid., p. 282.
13. Kowalski, *Goodbye Friend*, pp. 126-127.

Chapter Eleven
1. Lorenz, *Man Meets Dog*, p. 24.
2. Suso, *The Little Book of Eternal Wisdom*.
3. Saunders, *Beautiful Joe*, p. 238.

Chapter Twelve
1. Anderson, *Angel Animals*, p. xxii.
2. Kowalski, *The Souls of Animals*, p. 19.
3. Vesey-Fitzgerald, *Animal Anthology*.
4. Scanziani, *Enciclopedia del Cane*, p. 193.
5. Garber, *Dog Love*, p. 34.
6. Morris, *My Dog Skip*, p. 38.

Chapter Thirteen
1. Coren, *Why We Love The Dogs We Do*, p. 18.
2. Fouts, *Next of Kin: What Chimpanzees Have Taught Me about Who We Are*.
3. Wilson, *The Biophilia Hypothesis*.
4. Ibid.
5. Dodman, *The Dog Who Loved Too Much*, p. 18.
6. Ibid., p. 20.
7. Smith, *Pet Souls: Evidence that Animals Survive Death*.

Chapter Fourteen
1. Keats. *The Letters of John Keats*.
2. Schoen, *Kindred Spirits*, pp. 4-9.
3. McElroy, *Animals as Teachers and Healers*, p. 147.
4. Masson, *Dogs Never Lie About Love*, p. 43.

Chapter Fifteen
1. Levine, *Healing Into Life and Death*, p. 4.
2. ASPCA, *Animal Watch*, Spring 2001, p. 29.
3. Ibid., p. 31.
4. Ibid.
5. His Holiness the Dalai Lama and Cutler, *The Art of Happiness*, p. 79.
6. McElroy, *Animals As Guides For The Soul*, pp. 131-133.
7. Saunders, *Beautiful Joe*, p. 192.
8. Welshons, *Awakening from Grief*, p. 93.

ABOUT THE AUTHOR

D. J. Filson has enjoyed a lifetime of close involvement with animals. She was raised on a cattle ranch in western Montana, and her early childhood was spent participating in every aspect of ranch living. Her long-standing association with dogs is a part of her earliest memories. These alliances have provided a mutual realm of well-being, from life-saving rescues to sublime support.

Throughout her career as a social worker, she has witnessed the significance that dogs and other pets play in the lives of children and adults who are at risk of being abused or neglected. At times, these relationships provide one of the few stable and trustworthy connections that many individuals have in their lives. The comfort and security provided by these loyal and loving companions give a sense of stability and balance to vulnerable and lonely individuals and help mitigate patterns of chaos and distrust.

D.J. Filson graduated from the School of Social Work at the University of Montana and is currently a supervisor in child protective services. She also studied photography at Montana State University. She has published articles on the western lifestyle and has won numerous awards as a photographer. She is a descendent of John Filson, Kentucky author and historian, whose chronicles about Daniel Boone eventually made Boone famous both in the United States and Europe. She lives in western Montana where she shares her home with two lively terriers, Scotia and Dundee. This is her first book.